Unexpected Night

by Elizabeth Daly

1940

...eventful unexpected night,
Which finishes a row of plotting days,
Fulfilling their designs.

Death's Jest-Book; or The Fool's Tragedy
Thomas Lovell Beddoes

CHAPTER ONE
A Pale Young Man

Pine trunks in a double row started out of the mist as the headlights caught them, opened to receive the car, passed like an endless screen, and vanished. The girl on the back seat withdrew her head from the open window.

"We'll never get there at this rate," she said. "We're crawling."

The older woman sat far back in her corner, a figure of exhausted elegance. She said, keeping her voice low: "In this fog, I don't think it would be safe to hurry."

"I should think it would be safer than keeping him up all night."

"We'll see what Hugh thinks."

But the speaker did not move immediately. She looked too tired to move. Her face, under the short veil and the close black hat, showed white in the dimness, of the same whiteness as the small pearls in her ears. Presently she leaned forward, her high-collared woollen coat falling softly away and showing the dark silk dress beneath. She put a hand in a white glove on the back of the driver's seat.

"Can we go a little faster, Hugh?" she asked. "It's so late."

"It's this fog."

"I think it's only what they call a sea turn, up here; it will blow over before morning."

"Scares me to death. I don't know the road, and we don't want any bumps."

"Is he all right?" She peered anxiously at what looked like a heap of rugs beside the driver—a heap surmounted by a Panama hat. It stirred, and she asked: "Are you all right, Amby?"

A voice replied, drowsily: "All right. Been having a nap." It added, rather crossly: "Don't be feeble, Hugh. Step on it."

The car picked up speed.

"I'm sorry if I waked you, dear." The woman's voice was calm and cheerful, but her gloved hand gripped the edge of the seat in front. "Would you like another little drink of brandy?"

"No, thanks, Aunt El. Don't worry about me." The words were polite, but the tone was dry. "I'll make it."

She sat back, resting her head, trimly encased in the small hat, against the back of her seat. The young man called Hugh kept his eyes on the road, but he nudged the other with an elbow, and slightly shook his head. A face, which had until now been almost entirely hidden between the turned-down hat brim and the turned-up collar of a heavy topcoat, looked upwards and caught the light. It had fine dark eyes, but in all other respects it resembled a death mask that had been tinted blue, even to the lips. It spoke, with amiable irony:

"Calm yourself; I'll be good."

"You'd better be, old boy."

"I get so sick of all the fussing."

"You ought to be grateful for it."

"This 'bring 'em back alive' business gets on my nerves."

"It gets on my nerves when you talk that rot. Insulting people that care for you!"

"Invalids always get that way. Didn't you know?"

"You've been spoiled. If you were well, I'd take it out of you. You think you can say anything."

"That's because I can't do anything. It gets on my nerves."

"You and your nerves. If you had any nerves, you wouldn't be planning this crazy trip, to-morrow."

"I'm going, if it's the last thing I do."

"I ought to tell your aunt about it."

"She couldn't stop me. I'll be of age—don't forget that."

"I'm not likely to forget it; you don't talk about anything else." The young man paused, and then said, slowly: "You know I don't run people down, as a rule; but if Atwood had any decency, he wouldn't let you try it."

"He's all right. He doesn't keep on lecturing me, anyway."

"What's a tutor for?"

"You won't be a tutor much longer."

"Don't remind me of it. I'm trying to get in a few last licks, to-night."

The boy hesitated, and then said persuasively: "You know I've asked you again and again to come up there with me."

"Go barnstorming with you in that summer theatre? Certainly not. I haven't taken leave of my senses."

"There's nothing crazy about a summer theatre."

"There is for you. Look here, Amby; why not let me drive on straight to the hotel? It's getting on to midnight. You must be pretty well done up after that bad turn you had to-day, and your aunt and sister are half dead."

"I'm always having bad turns; one, more or less, makes no difference to me. Fred's expecting us."

"I can telephone down from the hotel, and say you didn't feel up to it."

"No. I want to see him."

"And the doctor says you mustn't be thwarted. How you trade on that, young fellow!"

The pale young man, hunched to the ears in his topcoat, chuckled. His sister spoke from the back seat, after drawing her head in at the car window: "That Ford hasn't passed us yet."

"What Ford?" The driver glanced back.

"It's been following us for miles."

The pale young man turned to look at her face, which showed, a white blur, in the car's dark interior. Then he, also, craned out of his window. When he drew his head in, he said cheerfully: "You're crazy. Here she comes, now."

A horn sounded, and the small car passed them. Its driver, a small man in a sou'wester much too big for him, flashed by and vanished in the mist ahead. The boy laughed, teasingly. "No holdups to-night," he said. "Poor old Alma. No excitement."

"We're almost there." His aunt leaned forward to look out of the car. "Yes, just a minute or two more. Turn right, Hugh, and then straight along the shore road. The Barclay cottage is the second on the left."

The screen of trees had rolled up at last. They were in the open, rumbling across a wooden bridge; a salt smell came from the marshes on either hand, but the fog closed in now like a barrage. The car slowed down.

"This is bad," said the driver.

"Only a minute more, Hugh. The second cottage on the left."

The Barclay cottage, a gabled relic of the eighties, was situated rather bleakly on the outskirts of a small summer resort called Ford's Beach. Its only small, dry front yard, a sandy road, and a low rampart of rock were all that separated it from the ocean. It was also rather bleak within. Its combination lobby, living and dining-room—walled, ceiled and floored with native pine—was made cheerful by a log fire, and a faded Navajo blanket on a couch in one corner; there was no other brightness or colour, no pictures, no knick-knacks, and no flowers.

Four persons sat around a bridge table, in the glare of a droplight: Colonel and Mrs. Barclay, their son, Lieutenant Frederic Barclay, and a guest from the hotel, a Mr. Henry Gamadge. The time was twenty minutes to twelve o'clock, and the date was Sunday night, June 25, 1939.

The three men were adding up scores; Mrs. Barclay was digging small change out of the cavernous recesses of a large knitting bag. She looked, and was, an old campaigner. As an Army wife she had learned to travel light, and had forever lost the habit of collecting bric-a-brac, or of regarding her home as anything more permanent than officer's quarters in a camp or barracks. Mrs. Barclay liked to think that she was a cosmopolitan, and had somehow acquired the notion that this involved wearing a curled fringe or bang, and piling the rest of her light hair high on the top of her head. She also felt obliged to dress formally in the evening, no matter what the circumstances; grudging exception being made in the case of picnics and dining-cars. On this occasion she wore a limp, flowered costume, cut very low; a fluttering chiffon scarf; and several strings of Venetian glass beads.

She was tall, thin, and very strong. Her game of golf was formidable, but she ruined her score on the approaches and the greens. She drove the family car much as she had once ridden a horse—sitting very straight, and bumping very much.

Colonel Barclay was a short, round man with a sunburned face and a clipped grey moustache. He was immaculate, if a little shabby, in yellowing white flannel trousers and a tight, blue serge coat. His son, Lieutenant Frederic Barclay, was also immaculate, and also shabby; but the resemblance between them went no farther. Lieutenant Barclay, Field Artillery, stationed in the South, and now spending his leave (for economy's sake) with his parents, was a tall, broad-shouldered and extremely handsome young man. He had long, dark, sleepy-looking eyes, smooth, dark hair, and a clear skin, slightly tanned. He moved slowly and deliberately, without effort; and he looked presentable in anything.

Mr. Henry Gamadge, on the other hand, wore clothes of excellent material and cut; but he contrived, by sitting and walking in a careless and lopsided manner, to look presentable in nothing. He screwed his grey tweeds out of shape before he had worn them a week, he screwed his mouth to one side when he smiled, and he screwed his eyes up when he pondered. His eyes were greyish green, his features blunt, and his hair mouse-coloured. People as a rule considered him a well-mannered, restful kind of young man; but if somebody happened to say something unusually outrageous or inane, he was wont to gaze upon the speaker in a wondering and somewhat disconcerting manner.

He said now, writing something on his score pad, and drawing a circle around it, "It's getting a little late. Shall we go on, or shall we have the return rubber another night? Perhaps you'll play with me to-morrow, at the Ocean House."

"Going on midnight." The colonel looked up at his watch. "We'll have to wait up," he grumbled, "but we'll let you off, if you like."

"I have an early golf match to-morrow, or I wouldn't suggest stopping. I'm afraid I'm the big winner."

Mrs. Barclay fished a heap of small change out of her knitting bag. "I don't feel like any more bridge to-night," she said. "Let me see, Mr. Gamadge. At a twentieth of a cent, I must owe you a dollar."

"That's right, Mrs. Barclay; but it can stand over."

"No, indeed. My father always said, 'Never get up from the bridge table owing money.' I should be the winner, really."

"Yes. Hard luck."

"I suppose it was mad to redouble the spades, but I was counting on Freddy. He is such a good holder, usually. I was counting on him."

"Lots of psychology in family bridge." Her son subdued a yawn. "How far am I down, Gamadge?"

"You're up thirty cents. Thirty cents to your offspring, Colonel."

"Come across, Dad."

Colonel Barclay heaved himself sidewise in his chair, got two dimes and two nickels out of his trouser pocket, and shoved them over the khaki bridge-table cover towards his son. "You'll be wanting to get to bed, Gamadge," he said, "if you have a nine o'clock golf match."

"I have, sir; with old Mr. Macpherson from Montreal."

"But you must wait and have a nightcap with us. I was sure the Cowdens would be here long before this."

"They couldn't make it much earlier than twelve, leaving Portsmouth at about ten," said young Barclay. "Sanderson telephoned from there, you know. He said he was going to drive slowly."

"Eleanor must be mad," complained Mrs. Barclay. "Ridiculous to stop here. Not that it isn't very sweet of your cousin to want to see you, Freddy. Still, to-morrow would do."

"'To-morrow' isn't a date he can be sure of keeping, you know, Mum."

"My dear child! And don't you give him his present to-night, whatever you do. It's very unlucky to give birthday presents before the day."

"He'll think he's very unlucky to get this one, whenever he gets it."

"Now, Freddy; a lovely case, for his medicated cigarettes! The prettiest one in the gift shop."

"He has one, and it came from Bond Street, I think. Or Cartier's."

"This will be just the thing for ordinary use. It's such a sad story, Mr. Gamadge; really a tragedy."

"Your nephew is so very seriously ill?"

"Incurably so. It's his heart. He had rheumatic fever while he was quite a child, and the aftereffects were very serious. He cannot live long. He has these attacks more and more often; he had one to-night, just before they reached Portsmouth. But he insisted on coming along to-night."

"Curious that his people should allow it," said Gamadge.

"They don't cross him," said the Colonel. "They do as he pleases. He should have been brought up to obey orders."

"Now, Father, it's easy to say that, but it has been a dreadful problem for poor Eleanor; my sister-in-law, Mr. Gamadge—she's his guardian; his parents are dead. My brother was appointed guardian to both the children, and then he died, and now Eleanor looks after them."

"Two children, are there?"

"Oh, yes. Brother and sister."

"Alma doesn't count—yet," said young Barclay, smiling a little.

"Of course she counts, Freddy! What a thing to say!"

"You'll have to tell Gamadge all about it, Mum; he looks interested."

Gamadge was glad that he had given that impression. He said: "There's a story, is there?"

"A very interesting story, Mr. Gamadge. A very peculiar story. My nephew Amberley will be twenty-one years old to-morrow, and he will come into nearly a million dollars."

"Whew!"

"If he lives," said young Barclay. He consulted his watch, and added: "Sixty-eight minutes to go. I should say he'd make it."

"Freddy!"

"Well, Mum, we're all pretty well used to the situation by this time. Matter of fact, he may live for years."

"It *is* an interesting situation, though," said Gamadge. "May I ask what would have happened to the million if he hadn't lived?"

"That's what makes it so interesting," said young Barclay, in a dry tone. "Every cent of it would go to some French connections that none of us has ever laid eyes on."

An ancient grievance was smouldering in Mrs. Barclay's eye. She said crossly: "I still think that will could have been broken. I said at the time that it could have been broken. I begged and implored Mr. Ormville—that's our lawyer, Mr. Gamadge—I begged him——"

The Colonel spoke rather impatiently: "Ormville knows what can and can't be done, Lulu. The will was all right."

"It was iniquitous! My oldest sister, Mr. Gamadge, was eccentric; I still think that she had become irresponsible."

"Mum was ready and willing to shoot her into a lunatic asylum, weren't you, poor old Mum?" laughed Fred Barclay.

"I certainly should have done something about it if I had known; but we didn't know, unfortunately, Mr. Gamadge… until she died. You see, she had married a Frenchman, and she had lived in France for years. She had become very peculiar even before she died. She didn't care for any of us any more—her own relations!—except my brother, Amberley's father. He took the child over there to see her, and she immediately took a fancy to the child. It amounted to infatuation."

"And you took this child over to see her, and she took anything but a fancy to me," laughed Fred Barclay.

Mrs. Barclay ignored him. "Amberley has stayed with her several times. She took him to specialists. She gave him a huge allowance. And when she died, she left a will leaving him all her money—if he should live to be twenty-one years old. If he didn't, it was to go to her husband's French relations."

"I see," said Gamadge. "It was her husband's money, was it?"

"Oh, yes; he was a very rich man. Some of them are, you know—they make it in Indo-China, or somewhere. I thought him very vulgar."

"Not at all," growled the Colonel. "Good sort of fellow."

"You should see his relations, Harrison! You never met them, but I did. Freddy is wrong when he says none of us has ever laid eyes on them. I did, years ago."

"Mother has met everybody, at one time or another," said young Barclay, shuffling the cards.

"But they weren't anybody, Fred. Well, that's how it is, Mr. Gamadge. Can you imagine the strain it has all been for poor Eleanor Cowden, my sister-in-law?"

Fred Barclay burst out laughing. "You're a caution, Mum. No wonder the lot of you have turned poor old Amby into a cynic."

"You know perfectly what I mean, dear, and it is very wrong of you to take that attitude. We are all devoted to Amberley, Mr. Gamadge. His illness has been a great anxiety to us all. Of course it has warped him a little; it would be a miracle if it hadn't. But everybody tells me that Mr. Sanderson—that's his tutor, Mr. Gamadge—has done wonders for the child's morale."

"He plays the deuce with mine, though." Young Barclay tilted his chair back against the wall. "Makes me tired. 'Doesn't your sister need a change of air after her cold? Have some consideration for your dear aunt.' That sort of thing."

"Mr. Sanderson is not at all like that, Freddy. If it were not for him, Amberley would be spoiled—utterly spoiled. He was beginning to think of nothing and nobody but himself. I was surprised and delighted when you told me about his making that will."

"Another source of strain," said Fred Barclay, glancing at Gamadge. "He can't make a will until tomorrow, of course; but he's got one all written out and ready to sign."

"Three witnesses are required in this state, dear; don't forget that," begged Mrs. Barclay.

"Perhaps Gamadge will oblige; and you and Dad. The rest of the family are beneficiaries," said her son. "There's only one shadow to mar the rosy prospect, Mum; he's sure to have left a slice—and a big one—to Arthur Atwood."

"Oh, dear!" sighed Mrs. Barclay.

The Colonel drummed on the table. "I don't want to hear a word more about this," he said, angrily. "It's repulsive."

"But, dear," protested his wife, "we all know that Arthur Atwood is perfectly horrible."

"Arthur Atwood," explained Fred Barclay, for Gamadge's benefit, "is the son of Mother's next most eccentric sister. So there you have the whole family; and we might as well include poor old Alma, insignificant as she seems, because if Amberley dies intestate she'll get all his money; unless he manages to give it away first. I shouldn't be surprised if he did. He's dying to get his hands on the principal. You can understand that he hasn't been able to raise a cent on his expectations."

"Of course not. Too bad a life," said Gamadge.

"No insurance, no borrowing, no anything. He's had this big allowance, though, and we've all been battening on it."

"Generous with it, is he?"

"In his own way."

"Haven't his aunt and his sister any money of their own?"

"Not much—have they, Dad?"

"None of us has had much since 1929." The Colonel got up. "I believe I hear the car."

Mrs. Barclay arose, and hastily followed her husband out on the porch. Young Barclay strolled after them. The open door let in a gush of damp air. Gamadge, whose interest in the arrivals had been considerably aroused, listened to the slamming of car doors, the chorus of greeting, the noise of many footsteps on gravel and then on wood. A crowd surged into the room.

"You must all be chilled to the bone. Come in, come in and get warm," trumpeted the Colonel. "Hot or cold drinks—all ready." He disappeared into the pantry.

Mrs. Barclay advanced, her arm in that of a tall, slender figure, beautifully dressed; her son followed more slowly, his arm about the shoulders of a smaller, slighter young man, beside whom a light-haired youth in a raincoat hovered anxiously. A dark girl brought up the rear of the procession. She stood for a moment or two in the doorway, and then closed the door and went over to a window. As she leaned there, looking out at the opaque curtain of mist beyond, Gamadge thought that she seemed neglected, unhappy and forlorn. She was rather casually dressed in a dark-blue flannel skirt, a rose-coloured blouse, and a leather coat. She wore no hat. Her dark hair, cut very short, lay as smoothly as a cap on her small head.

Young Barclay and the man in the raincoat had shepherded their charge to the fire, and were relieving him of his heavy tweed ulster, his white silk scarf, and his fine Ecuadorian Panama. Mrs. Barclay seized Gamadge's arm.

"Mr. Gamadge, I should like to introduce you to my sister-in-law, Mrs. Cowden. Eleanor, this is Mr. Gamadge, a friend of Fred's."

"How do you do?" said Mrs. Cowden, smiling. Gamadge saw that Mrs. Barclay had been right—Mrs. Cowden could smile and be civil, but she was indeed suffering from strain.

"How do you do?" he said. "You must be tired."

"We all are, a little."

"And this," said Mrs. Barclay, still gripping Gamadge's arm, and drawing him towards the fire, "this is my nephew. Dear Amberley. And Mr. Sanderson, who takes such good care of him."

The sudden modulation of her tone from affection to condescension might well have cut an oversensitive person like a knife; but Mr. Sanderson seemed to be philosophical; his thin, good-looking face registered nothing but polite good humour. He had turned from his charge, and was steering in the direction of Miss Cowden and the window. Mrs. Barclay said:

"Oh—there is dear Alma. I want you to meet Alma, Mr. Gamadge. I didn't see you, dear. This is Mr. Gamadge."

Alma Cowden nodded.

"Are you comfortable, Amby? Getting warm?" Mrs. Barclay dropped Gamadge's arm, and returned to the fireplace. "Fred, where is Amby's cocoa?"

Fred went into the pantry, and Gamadge went up to the young man who stood in front of the hearth. He had been prepared for symptoms of serious illness, but nothing could have prepared him for the skim-milk translucence of the face that smiled up at him. Its dark eyes looked like onyx against that pallor.

"Are you an old-timer here, Mr. Gamadge?" he asked.

"I think I may say so. I've been coming every summer for years."

"This is my first trip. Have you ever been up to a place called Seal Cove?"

"I've missed that."

"They tell me it's quite a short trip—just a few miles beyond Oakport. I have a cousin up there, this summer; he's helping to run a summer theatre."

"Interesting job."

"It opens to-morrow night. I wouldn't miss it for anything. Do you go to summer theatres much?"

"Well, to tell you the truth, not unless somebody hauls me. I must admit I like winter ones best."

The boy laughed, gaily. "This one is going to be better than most. They've got a manager that used to be with the Abbey Theatre—you know. I've met him. He's crazy about the Irish drama. Do you like the Irish drama, Mr. Gamadge?"

"Hang it all," said Gamadge, "I seem to be a complete blight, this evening. I *don't* care so very much about it, to be perfectly frank; but then, I haven't read all of it, or seen much of it. Perhaps I haven't given it a chance."

"Why don't you come up and try it at Seal Cove?" Young Cowden's face assumed a gleeful and impish expression. "I have an interest in drumming up audiences, you know. I'm…"

He had pulled off a pair of thick chamois gloves, and was twisting them into a rope. As his cousin appeared with a tray, he shoved them into a pocket, and produced a truly magnificent cigarette case. It was thin, made of platinum, and initialled in gold. "I won't offer you a cigarette," he said; "I only smoke those awful things without any tobacco in them."

"Without any nicotine, you mean, you young ass." Fred Barclay put the tray down on a stand, and poured out a cup. "Have some of this stuff, Alma?"

Alma Cowden, followed by Sanderson, came up to them.

"Don't look so cross," said her brother.

"I'm not cross."

"Cross as a bear all day. Isn't that so, Hugh?"

"Stop badgering your sister, and give me one of those gaspers of yours. I rather like them."

"I don't." Miss Cowden, ignoring young Barclay's proffered case, fished a crumpled package of cigarettes from her pocket. Sanderson gave her a light. He, too, was a little threadbare; his Harris tweeds had seen better days. In fact, of all the men in the room, the sick boy alone looked, and unconsciously behaved, like a rich man. "The heir," Gamadge reflected, "and his poor relations. It leaps to the eye."

Colonel Barclay, tray in hand, pushed at the swing door with his foot. Gamadge went over, relieved him of his burden, and set it on the bridge table. This had been drawn up beside the couch where Mrs. Barclay sat in deep conversation with her sister-in-law.

"Family reunion," thought Gamadge. "I ought to go. A short drink, and I'm off." He helped the colonel to mix highballs, while the two ladies chatted, practically in his ear:

"Of course it is dreadful to have to let him do these things, Lulu; but he must be kept happy."

"I should have thought, though, that if this attack at Portsmouth was so serious——"

"All his attacks are serious. We got a room for him, and Hugh Sanderson got him to bed; but he would get up and come on to-night. All he can think of is this wretched summer theatre. It opens tomorrow night, and he is determined to be on hand."

"Because those Atwoods are there!"

"And a little girl called Baker. He adores it all."

"He never would have got into it if it hadn't been for the Atwoods."

"I tried my best to break up the intimacy; he's been cross with me ever since. But that studio of theirs in New York was so bad for him—the smoke, and the crowds, and the excitement. Poor child, he hasn't had much fun, of course. You don't know what a strain it's all been, these last years. Oh, thank you, Mr. Gamadge. That looks just right."

She took the glass from him, and sat back against the cushions to enjoy it. Gamadge, mixing Mrs. Barclay's drink, glanced at her with admiration. Fine bones, fine skin, level eyebrows over hazel eyes, beautiful figure, beautiful, simple clothes. She must be in her late forties, but with that physique she would always be good-looking. The rippling brown hair that showed under one side of her small hat had no grey in it, but he would swear it wasn't dyed. Just one of those lucky people that couldn't grow old.

Colonel Barclay came up, and drew a chair to Mrs. Cowden's side. "Sit down, Gamadge," he said, patting the back of another one.

"No, thank you, Colonel. I'll just swallow this, and then I must go."

"Can we give you a lift to the hotel?" asked Mrs. Cowden. "If you don't mind a lot of things falling all over your feet, there's plenty of room."

"Thank you very much, I have my small bus."

He finished his whisky, shook hands with her and with his host and hostess, and crossed the room. Miss Cowden had again retired to the window, and Mr. Sanderson had again joined her there. Lieutenant Barclay was handing a paper to Amberley Cowden, who said, as he shoved it into a pocket: "What do you think?"

"Fine. But you'll live to bury the lot of us."

"Don't be silly."

"Too bad Aunt El is in such a deuce of a hurry; you could have stayed here till the zero hour, and got it off your mind." He turned, as Gamadge came up. "Going, old man? I was just telling young Amberley that the state of Maine requires three witnesses to a will."

"Uncle and Aunt Lu and Mr. Gamadge could have signed; that's so. Well, to-morrow will do. Can't you wait and go up with us, Mr. Gamadge?"

"I have a little car outside. Good night, Mr. Cowden."

"Next time you see me, I'll be twenty-one."

"That so?"

"Yes. Goes by standard time." He consulted his watch. "It's only ten past eleven, really." He shook hands with Gamadge, who went over to the pair by the window. This time they were both contemplating the curtain of mist. When he spoke, they turned. Sanderson shook hands, amiably; but she did not at first seem to remember who Gamadge was, or why he was there. Her short, smooth dark hair, brushed straight back from her forehead, gave her a melancholy, Pierrot look, and her dark eyes met his with a brooding gaze.

"Good night, Miss Cowden."

"Good night."

He went out, turning up his collar; found his way across the yard to the road; stood for a moment admiring the big Cowden car, and then climbed into the modest coupé behind it, and drove off through the mist.

CHAPTER TWO
Gamadge Minds His Own Business

From the Barclay Cottage to the Ocean House drive the shore road rises gently, curving to the left. It then dips again, runs level for a couple of miles, and turns inland through pinewoods to Oakport Village. Gamadge would have said that he knew every bump of it; but to-night the fog had dropped a veil over the familiar and the real. It had muffled the sound of the tide that came booming in below the rocks on the right, so that the surf might have been half a mile away, instead of just across the beach. It had dimmed the lights of the cottages on the left, so that these were confused with the bathhouse and the beach shops, and Gamadge thought he had passed the boardwalk long before he had reached it. He nearly missed the turn to the hotel.

He backed, went up the rough drive, and followed it past the Ocean House down to the garage. Drawing up in front of the sign that said: "Please Do Not Blow Your Horn," he called Kimball, the night man.

"Don't bury my car behind the big one that's coming in," he begged.

"Lots of room, this early in the season," replied Kimball.

Gamadge walked up to the hotel, climbed the steps, crossed the wide veranda, and opened one of the doors that led into the lobby. These were usually wide, but to-night they were closed against the fog. Sam, the night watchman, sat behind the counter, his feet up, eating a banana.

"Hello, Mr. Gamadge," he said. "Nice night for a drive."

"Fine. I hope it blows over before morning."

"It'll blow over before that."

"Your party from New York is on the way. I just saw them down at the Barclays'."

"I'm all ready for 'em."

"Don't stare when you see the boy. He startles you, for a minute. He has heart trouble, you know, and it makes him a queer colour."

"I heard he was sick. How about my takin' him up in the elevator?"

"The what?"

"The freight elevator."

"Oh, that thing. I don't think they'd trust him on it. If they had to have an elevator for him, they'd have written and asked about one."

"Mrs. Cowden's been here before. She knows there ain't any."

"Have Waldo call me at eight, will you? I have a golf date."

"O.K." Sam made a note on a pad. Gamadge's eye wandered to the mailboxes, and he stared, unpleasantly affected by what he saw.

"Don't tell me there's a letter for me."

"Seems so. And a big one," replied Sam, taking it out of its pigeonhole, and handing it across the counter.

"Oh, Lord. Proof. I'll be at it an hour."

"Can't it wait till to-morrow?"

"No, it can't. I have to get it into the box for the early collection."

He climbed the first flight of wide, shallow stairs, and then the second, steeper one that led to his room on the second floor. He was as yet alone on this corridor, which somehow conveyed an impression of the fact, as hotel corridors mysteriously do, even without the testimony of dark, closed transoms and a minimum of light. Nobody had bothered to close the glass door at the end; it gave on the spiral stairway, enclosing the shaft of the freight elevator, that did duty at the Ocean House for fire escape. Salt air, damp and fog-laden, met Gamadge as he turned towards his room.

Should he close the end door? He decided against it, opened his own, and switched on his light. He took his coat off, sat down, put his feet up on the only other chair, got out his fountain pen, and went to work.

At five minutes past one Sam looked up from his magazine, saw the darkness beyond the glass of the front doors change to grey, to cloudy opalescence, to yellow. He jumped up, came from behind the counter, and hurried across the lobby and out on the porch. The Cowden car was just coming to a stop at the foot of the veranda steps. He ran down and opened the rear door.

"Glad to have you back, Mrs. Cowden," he said. "How are you?"

"Why, it's Sam. Nice to see you again. I've brought my family with me, this summer. This is my niece."

"How are you, Miss Cowden?" Sam helped the elder lady out, and would have done the same for the other; but she jumped down without his assistance, and ran up the steps and into the hotel, her little dressing case in her hand. The blond young man in the raincoat who had been behind the wheel slipped out, came around the car, and opened the near front door. Sam, getting out luggage, watched from the corner of his eye while he helped a bundled figure to descend, decided that his own help was not needed, and after one glimpse of the livid face between hat-brim and coat collar, turned away. When the bags were out, he put his fingers to his mouth and gave a low, owl-like hoot, which brought a similar response from the garage.

"Don't bother." The young man in the raincoat paused in his slow ascent of the steps, his arm in that of his companion. "I can drive the car down."

"No trouble. Kimball ain't busy." Sam started on his first trip into the hotel with the luggage, thinking: "They're all tuckered out, and three of 'em's scared to death. The sick feller ain't. Acts like he was enjoying it."

The pale young man had, in fact, straightened, thrown back his shoulders, shaken off Sanderson's arm, and looked about him with a cheerful smile. Mrs. Cowden, bringing up the rear with Sam, murmured: "My nephew isn't well."

"I heard he wasn't."

"We were terribly frightened on the way up from the Barclays'. He had some cocoa there. I don't think it agreed with him."

"That's too bad."

"I thought we should never get him here."

"Want I should call a doctor?"

"No, he says he's all right. But he always says that. Oh, dear! What is he doing now?"

The pale young man had walked across to the desk, and was writing in the register.

"Come off it, Amby," protested Sanderson. "No need for that. Come on up to bed."

Sam put the luggage on the floor, and went behind the counter to officiate. The young man looked up at him, and then, above his head, at the clock on the wall. He gave Sam a roguish and elfin smile.

"That clock of yours right?" he asked.

"Set it by radio every day."

"Then I've been of age for eleven minutes. This is my birthday."

"Many hap——" began Sam.

"I don't know about that; but I can do as I please, now, and I want to register." He finished his task, and Sam, blotting it, read, upside down:

Mrs. Francis Cowden,NewYorkCity. Miss Alma Cowden,"""" Amberley Cowden,""""
Hugh Sanderson,"""" "That right?"

"It's exactly right, Mr. Cowden."

"Any telephone message for me?"

Sam investigated in the rack, and said there was none.

"Funny. All right, Hugh. I'll go up, now. What's the hurry?"

Sanderson, who had been exchanging helpless glances with Mrs. Cowden, propelled the recalcitrant young man toward the stairs. Miss Cowden had been standing halfway up, her back turned to them all. Sam picked up three bags, and led the way to the first door.

"Right down here," he said, walking the length of the corridor, and stopping in front of a room just to the right of the fire-escape door. "Number 21—that's yours, Mrs. Cowden. Miss Cowden has 19, next door; bath between. Mr. Cowden is in 17, with bath. Mr. Sanderson is opposite, Number 20; single, no bath. That right?"

"That's right, thank you, Sam. Just bring the rest of the things up, and we'll settle ourselves in." She gave him a generous tip, and went through the door he held open for her. "Oh, how glad I am to be here. I suppose we could get at extra blankets? He—he's apt to be cold."

"Right in the linen closet, down the hall."

"We'll get them if we need them."

Sam deposited her bags in the room, opened the other doors, and then went down for the rest of the luggage. When he approached Room 17 with a handsome pigskin dressing case, he found the occupant sitting on the edge of the bed, bent over with his hands between his knees, and breathing hard. Sam's kind, freckled face was troubled.

"You all right?" he enquired, putting the case on the table.

"Yes. Fine. Call Sanderson, will you?"

Sam did so, and went downstairs. He had left the three golf bags belonging to the party leaning against the counter; he put them in the lobby chest, and was just emerging when the office telephone rang. He went back to answer it, and heard Sanderson's voice:

"That you, Sam? Hang on a minute."

"Yes, sir."

Sanderson's voice went on, to somebody else: "All right, Amby, you idiot. Go ahead, and make it short."

Sam said: "You want to make a call, Mr. Cowden?"

"Yes, I do. It's to Seal Cove. You know where that is?"

"Yes. Oakport exchange."

"I don't know the number, it's that summer theatre—'The Old Pier Players.'"

"I'll get the Oakport operator."

Sam got into communication with Oakport. Presently he said: "They have no telephone up there, Mr. Cowden."

"What? There must be one. That's crazy."

"No, sir, they haven't. No number listed."

"Perhaps they're all asleep. Ring them again."

"No number to ring."

"I don't understand. It's a theatre. They must have a telephone."

"Wait a minute." Sam again interviewed Oakport, and came back with the news: "They ain't installed yet. They only been there a week, and the poles was all down. There's been a lot of trouble with outlying districts since the storm last fall. Operator can get you Tucon."

"Where's that?"

"Little place on the back route from Oakport to Portland. They been getting their messages and telegrams left there in some store. Operator has the number. They might take your call, and ride down to the Cove with it."

"Oh, well; I hate to get them up, this time of night."

"It's only a little place. Might not anybody be around, late as this."

"I should think those people at the Cove would be wild."

"I should, too."

"Well, it's not so important as all that. I guess——"

Sanderson's voice said: "Amby, you are a jackass. I'll get him for you first thing in the morning. Now will you quit? I want to go to bed. I'm all in."

"I see now why there wasn't any message for me to-night."

"Of course. He couldn't get through. Quit, will you?"

"All right, Sam."

The receiver clicked. Sam exchanged some words with Oakport, and returned to his magazine. He was deep in it, when a curious sound on the stairs beside him made him look up, and then stare, transfixed. The sound had been, as he thought, laboured breathing.

He gazed incredulously at the pallid, smiling face, the tweed coat, the white silk muffler, the thick yellow chamois gloves, and the Panama hat; and he spoke as he had never before spoken to a guest of the Ocean House:

"What you doing down here?"

"Oh, you're there, are you? I wasn't sure you would be."

"Certainly I'm here."

"I thought you might be making your rounds. You do, don't you?"

"Yes, I do. You ain't going out, Mr. Cowden?"

"Not if you'll do something for me. I dropped my cigarette case. I had it in the car, and I know just where it must be—right outside, near the steps. It must have fallen out of my coat when Hugh Sanderson was helping me down."

Sam, remembering that awkward exit from the front seat, was not surprised to hear that something had been dropped in the process; but he continued to stare.

"Why didn't you telephone down?" he demanded. "Why didn't you send ____"

"Sanderson's dead on his feet; I'm as fresh as a daisy. I had two solid hours in bed, at Portsmouth."

"You could have telephoned."

"They're not asleep, yet. They might have heard me. I want my cigarette case; it's a good one."

"You were going poking out in this fog, lookin' for it? You must be crazy. You turn right round and go on back up to bed. I'll find it, if it's there." Sam got up, and produced a big torch from under the counter.

"All right. Keep your hair on. You can stick it in a drawer, till morning."

"I'd put it in the safe, only the safe's locked."

"Just stick it in a drawer."

"You go on up to bed. Your aunt will be crazy," said Sam, unconsciously using the tone that he would have employed for a bad boy, rather than a young man who had just come of age. He refused the dollar that was offered him over the banisters.

"I haven't found it yet," he said. "To-morrow will do." He went out, poked for some time about the roadway and the steps, and finally saw a grey, softly gleaming object in the rough grass that edged the drive. He turned it over, wondered at its subtle sheen, and went back into the hotel.

Relieved to see that the pale young man had disappeared, he went into the back office and bestowed the cigarette case in an envelope, and marked it. Then he shut the envelope carefully into a desk drawer. When he emerged, Gamadge was sliding a thick letter into the mail slot.

"See young Cowden?" asked Sam.

"No. What do you mean? Didn't they come long ago?"

"Sure they did." Sam glanced up at the clock, which said 1:40. "Half an hour. He came down again, just now."

"Shouldn't think they'd let him do that."

Sam explained. "I thought there was something funny about it," he said, looking bothered.

"How funny?"

"Can't exactly say. He was all bundled up."

"Well—he meant to go out in the fog, if you weren't here."

"He looked to me like he was goin' somewhere more than that."

"Where on earth should he be going, at this hour? And in his condition?"

"If he wasn't a sick feller, I'd have said he was goin' out to keep a date."

"Date! You must be dreaming. He doesn't know a soul in the place, so far as I can make out, except the Barclays."

"Well, I guess I am crazy; but he looked too much dressed up to be going out just to look for a cigarette case."

"Perhaps that heart trouble of his makes him cold. I think I've heard so." Gamadge turned towards the stairs and paused on the lowest step. "Come to think of it, Sam, it's his birthday."

"So he said."

"And it meant something to him, let me tell you! He's been a rich man for forty minutes."

Gamadge climbed to the first floor, and stood looking down the hall. Sam's story had impressed him; but he was inclined to think that they were both making too much of it.

"Hang it all," he thought, irresolute, his eyes wandering from one end of the silent corridor to the other. "I can't go knocking them up; they'd hear me, if I even scratched on his door. They must be down at that end—all the transoms are open. Shall I go back and get his room number from Sam? It does seem such a nursemaidy, rocking-chair thing to do. No, I won't. Nothing to it."

Gamadge, in fact, had a virtue that sometimes transformed itself into a fault; that of minding his own business. He went up to the second flight of stairs, into cold, fog-laden air; entered his room; and was in bed and asleep in ten minutes.

CHAPTER THREE
Not Much of a Birthday

A violent knocking finally persuaded Gamadge to open his eyes. The room was flooded with sunshine. "All right, all right," he muttered.

Waldo, the tall bellboy, put his head around the door. "I forgot to call, Mr. Gamadge. It's nearly nine."

"Good Lord, Macpherson will be raging." Gamadge sat up annoyed. "What's the idea, forgetting your calls?"

"We're all upset. It don't matter about Mr. Macpherson, he's down at the cliff."

"Where?"

"Down the road, on the lookout. Something terrible happened. One of the guests fell off the rocks."

"That's too bad. When? This morning?"

"Last night. Young feller that just checked in. Name's Cowden."

"Cowden!" Gamadge suddenly came awake. "Yes, sir. They think he had a heart attack, and fell over the cliff. Everybody's down there. They just took the remains away."

Gamadge, staring at the bellboy, swung one leg over the side of the bed. "What did he go down there for?"

"They don't know."

"Do they know when it happened?"

"Somebody said around two o'clock."

Gamadge groaned. "Who found him?"

"One of the gypsies from the camp down in the grove. Kid named Stanley. He was out on the beach early, about seven, picking up driftwood and jelly seaweed before the beach cleaners got around. The body had a typewritten name and address pinned inside the coat; case of accidents."

"Of course. So somebody telephoned here?"

"They got hold of Mr. Sanderson—he's a feller came with the Cowden party. He went and got the Barclays—they're some relation of the feller that got killed. The sheriff sent a detective over, and he's grilling Sam Leavitt."

"I didn't know the sheriff had a detective."

"Some friend of his; state detective, or something. He wants to see you, Mr. Gamadge; that's how I remembered about your call."

"Thanks very much." Gamadge swung the other leg to the floor. "Where is he?"

"Room 17—that's the room the Cowden feller had."

"You tell him I'll be there as soon as I've had a swallow of coffee. Tell him I want to be grilled, too."

Waldo rushed away. Gamadge had a quick bath, pulled on his clothes, and went down to the dining-room. At 9:40 he knocked at the door of Number 17.

"Come in," said a mild, slow voice. Gamadge entered, closed the door behind him, and looked down into the square face of a grey, stocky man who sat in a hard rocking chair. He wore a business suit, waistcoat and all, and black, shiny shoes. Sam was perched on a hard chair opposite him. He looked puzzled and upset, and he evidently needed sleep; otherwise, his grilling did not seem to have had serious effects on him.

"Mr. Gamadge," he exclaimed, "ain't this awful?"

"Yes, it is."

"You just missed him. If you'd seen him, you might have felt the way I did, and gone after him, or something."

"I might have." He nodded to the grey man, who nodded in return. "I'm Mitchell," he said.

"How do you do?" Gamadge's eyes wandered around the small, neat room, which showed no signs of occupancy except a dressing gown and a pair of pyjamas lying on the bed, a closed suitcase on the floor, and a closed pigskin dressing case on the table. "Did they pull you out of bed, Sam?" he asked.

"No; I hadn't gone to bed. I don't get relieved till 7:30."

"First-class witness, Leavitt is," said Mitchell. "Mr. Gamadge: What about this cocoa?"

"Cocoa." Gamadge's eyes roved about the room again, and came back to Mitchell. "Cocoa?" he asked, with polite blankness.

"Sam Leavitt tells me the deceased had cocoa at Colonel Barclay's cottage last night, and was sick afterwards."

"Mis' Cowden said so. She said he was sick coming up here in the car, an' it must have been the cocoa."

"I remember, now. Young Cowden and his sister had cocoa. The rest of us were accommodated with whisky."

"His sister had some, did she?" Mitchell looked at Sam. "Did it disagree with her, too?"

"Not as far as I could see. She was spry enough. Grabbed her little suitcase, jumped out of the car, and skipped right up the steps and into the lobby. She wasn't sick."

"How'd the boy act? Didn't seem to be in pain, or anything?"

"He was fine, once the other feller got him out of the car. I thought first he was kind of weak, and I whistled Kimball up from the garage, so the feller wouldn't have to leave him. But afterwards you wouldn't have known he was sick, if it hadn't been for his colour, and his hard breathin'. He come over to the desk, and looked up at the clock, and started jokin' about it bein' his birthday. Lively as anybody."

"Well, thanks, Sam. That's all for now. You go on to bed."

Sam went; Gamadge sat down on the chair he had vacated, and lighted a cigarette. When he looked up, Mitchell's small blue eyes were on him.

"You know any of these people well, Mr. Gamadge?" he asked.

"I met the Cowdens last night, for the first time. The Barclays I know as summer acquaintances." He added, "I don't think there was anything the matter with their cocoa, Mitchell. I don't think Mrs. Cowden meant that there was."

"The boy being tired, and sick, anyway, it might have upset him. That the idea?"

"I think that was the idea."

"Of course we have to have an inquest." Mitchell spread out his hands, and contemplated his square fingers.

"I suppose you do."

"Our medical examiner seems to think that the deceased died of this heart trouble he had."

"And fell off the cliff during the attack?"

"Yes. We'd like to get hold of some kind of a working theory about why he went down there, in his condition, at that time of night."

"That cigarette-case business certainly points to a planned affair."

"I don't think there's any doubt but what it was. There seems to be some idea in the family that he was going for good."

"Really? Going where?"

"Up to a place called Seal Cove, where they have a summer theatre. He has a cousin up there."

"So he told me. He was interested in the place. But——"

"Sanderson tells me he was planning to go up to-day. You know he was having his twenty-first birthday?"

"Yes; I heard about that."

"All of it?"

"If you mean the financial situation, the Barclays told me about it last night."

"Not much of a birthday," said Mitchell, again spreading his hands and examining the fingers.

"And he was looking forward to it, too."

"Was, was he?"

"All kinds of plans. He was going to sign his will, to-day."

"It's missing."

"Is it, really? He put it in his pocket—I saw him; if that was the document he showed Fred Barclay."

"If it ain't there," Mitchell jerked his head towards the pigskin dressing case; "it ain't anywhere."

"How very odd."

"You'd think he'd take a thing like that case with him, if he was going off for good."

"He wouldn't have been able to carry anything, Mitchell. I know he'd never think of such a thing. But if he was going off for good, and didn't want his family to know it, why did he struggle through that cigarette-case comedy with Sam, instead of quietly decamping by way of the fire escape? It's only one flight down, and the dining-room and kitchens are at that end of the hotel. Not a soul would have seen him."

"He might not have known about the fire escape; and even if he did, he had a good reason for not going that way. He'd have had to pass his tutor's room, his sister's room, and his aunt's room; and even if they were in bed, the transoms were open."

"They were; I saw them."

"And those people hadn't hardly time to get to bed, much less to sleep. One squeak out of his shoes, or anything like that, and the trip was off."

"So it was."

"I'm going into all this, Mr. Gamadge, for two reasons. First, they think this cousin of his, Atwood, must have planned to drive down from the Cove, last night, and meet him at the cliff, and take him up there to that summer theatre. 'The Old Pier Players'; that's what the name is. Now, this Atwood hasn't come forward; so I'm going up there to see him. If there was any kind of an accident, down on the rocks, he may not want to admit being there; but we found a folding cheque book in the boy's pocket, and one of the cheques in it was made out to Atwood, and signed. Made out for one hundred dollars. It was folded right back with the others, and anybody going through his pockets would be likely to miss it. Now, Colonel Barclay tells me you're interested in handwriting, and ink, and so on, Mr. Gamadge."

"I am; trouble is, the handwriting and ink I'm interested in is usually from one to two hundred years old."

"Don't say!" Mitchell looked disappointed. "My idea was that perhaps you could tell whether that cheque was made out last night. If it was, you could argue that the deceased meant to *give* it to Atwood, last night."

"You could." Gamadge looked round at the immaculate blotter on the desk, and the brand-new steel pen. Mitchell said:

"There ain't a mark on that blotter, and no other blotter was in the room. He had a fountain pen—empty."

"Oh. Well, Mitchell, there's a faint, feeble possibility that I could tell you whether the ink on that cheque is Ocean House ink."

Mitchell's eye lighted.

"Don't count on it. If I can, it will be a lucky break. And I have no materials here to work with."

"I'll get 'em for you from Portland. The other request I have to make is this: You saw all these people, Mr. Gamadge; and you're the only person outside the family, except Sam, that did see 'em. I'd like to hear what you thought of 'em."

"That's a long order, on such a short acquaintance, I can tell you more or less what I thought of the boy himself; he was very attractive."

Mitchell raised his eyebrows. "Sam says he looked like a livin' corpse."

"His colour was startling, but otherwise he had a very attractive personality. His illness had warped him, I suppose; he was obviously spoiled; selfish, perhaps; self-indulgent; a trifle too used to having all the money in the outfit. But he had character. His illness hadn't made him morbid, he wasn't peevish, and he had (as you know already) physical and moral courage. I should say he was affectionate and generous to people he liked; and I should say he liked a good many people. I liked him, Mitchell. I hoped he'd get a little fun out of his money."

There was a pause. Then Mitchell said, woodenly: "Sheriff doesn't like the job of asking these bereaved ladies questions."

"No; very unpleasant. So he passed the buck to you."

"I don't like it any better than he does."

"What questions do you want to ask them, anyway?"

Mitchell glanced at him, glanced out of the window, and said: "There'll be a post mortem."

"Naturally."

"What's more, there's a Doctor Ethelbert Baines in the hotel, and they say he's a big man in New York."

"He is. A very big man."

"He's a friend of the Cowdens. He's going over to the Centre to check up on Cogswell's findings."

"You couldn't have a better opinion."

"He had to die sometime soon, they tell me," continued Mitchell. "Nothing specially funny about his dying last night, after all he'd been through yesterday. He had a bad attack at Portsmouth."

Gamadge surveyed him for some moments in silence. Then, smiling faintly, he leaned back in his chair, stretched out his legs, gazed at the ceiling, and said reflectively; "What if they find some ante-mortem bruises? Or what if they don't? Having some imagination, it worries you a little to consider how soon he died after coming into his money. You can't help realising that if he had lived only a short time longer, he would have been living among new friends, spending his fortune on them, perhaps even getting married. You reflect morosely on the fact that his sister is his sole heir, since he doesn't seem to have got that will signed and witnessed. Is she his sole heir, Mitchell?"

"Yes, she is. But I don't——"

"You don't feel like going into the next room and asking her if she pushed her brother off the cliff, last night. That would certainly have given him a fatal heart attack, wouldn't it?"

Mitchell gave him a doubtful and grudging look. "I haven't said any such thing."

"So I had to say it for you. You want me to introduce you to these ladies?"

"I have to go easy."

"Certainly. The approach will have to be indirect."

"You mean you'll do it?"

"Certainly I'll do it. Why not?" Gamadge turned, and was about to pick up the telephone.

"Look out!" Mitchell started forward. "I have some fingerprint men coming down this afternoon."

"Oh." Gamadge picked the receiver up by its edge. "That you, Wilks? Give me—no, wait a minute. Send one of the boys up, will you?" He said over his shoulder: "Mrs. Cowden may not be answering her telephone."

"In a hurry, ain't you?" Mitchell studied him curiously, as he replaced the receiver on its hook.

"Aren't you?"

"I have to see Mrs. Barclay, and get up to the Cove."

"I'll drive you up, if you're agreeable. I'd like to see the place. The poor little beggar asked me to go. I think I'd do well to accept his invitation."

Peabody, the short bellboy, knocked and came in.

"Oh, Peabody," said Gamadge. "Go to Mrs. Cowden's door, will you, and ask her if she will speak to Mr. Gamadge on the telephone."

"Yes, sir."

"If she says she doesn't know who I am, tell her I'm a friend of the Barclays. She met me there last night."

Peabody walked solemnly down the hall, past the intervening room, to Number 21. They heard his knock, and a low-voiced conversation. He returned, his solemn face lighted by an unaccustomed smile. "She says yes."

"I don't believe that everybody could have got me that interview, Peabody. I'll remember it. Now go down and tell Wilks to put me on to Room 21. Tell him it's all right, Mrs. Cowden expects the call."

Peabody left, and Gamadge waited for a few moments, and then lifted the receiver again.

"Mrs. Cowden? I apologise for bothering you at such a time. First, let me ask if I can be of any help. Anything at all… Yes, I thought they might be at the Centre; that's why I… Let me know if there's anything, then. How is Miss Cowden?… Oh, I'm very sorry… You got hold of Baines? Good. I was going to say I could probably find him for you, on the golf course… Peabody did? That boy's a jewel.

"What I called up about, there's a man here from the sheriff's office, quite a nice fellow, state detective. He wants some data; you know these formalities. He didn't feel that he could bother you this morning, but I had an idea you might be willing to help him out. Of course he could wait for Colonel Barclay to get back from the Centre… You'll see him? I was pretty sure you would. Shall I get hold of him, then, and bring him up, say in half an hour? I agree with you—much better to get these things over with… Not at all, I'm only too glad. Good-bye."

Gamadge replaced the receiver gently on its hook, and turned to Mitchell with a condescending bow. Mitchell's answering look held a mild and questioning wonder.

"What's the matter?" asked Gamadge.

"You're a cool customer." Mitchell was amused. He went on, frowning: "Did she say Miss Cowden was sick?"

"Collapsed. They had Baines see to her."

"Now, that's too bad. I was counting on seeing her."

"You may, yet; who knows?"

Somebody knocked, and little Peabody made a second appearance, holding a large manila envelope as if it were a tea tray.

"State policeman just brought it," he said, and backed out, more solemn than ever. Mitchell said: "I will say they were pretty quick, over there. Not so bad, for the Centre." He took out a photograph, glanced at it, handed it to Gamadge, and busied himself with a typewritten report.

The picture showed a figure that looked merely like garments, carelessly flung down, so insignificant was it, spread-eagled below towering rocks. A Panama hat lay near it, and its tweed topcoat was twisted away from one shoulder, as if torn off in the fall. The body lay face down; there were no injuries to be seen on the back of the head; but the upper half of the face was a black smear.

Gamadge looked at it, turned it this way and that, and studied it from all angles. Then he handed it to Mitchell.

"Take it away," he said. "I don't like it."

"You can imagine how the little feller that found it felt. Those gypsies are hard-boiled characters, even the children; but when he got hold of the beach cleaners, this Stanley boy was crying."

"I feel like crying myself."

"Here's the list of what young Cowden had in his pockets. No papers, except that cheque book, and a bill or two. They sent the cheque book; here it is."

"Must I handle it by the edges, too?"

"No, I got that printed. No prints on it but his."

Gamadge opened it, and unfolded the signed cheque, which had not been torn out; unless opened, it resembled all the blank ones. He studied it, while Mitchell continued:

"No driving licence, of course. A wallet with some stamps and thirty-four dollars in cash. Handkerchief. Pair of chamois gloves, rolled up. Little bottle of medicine—iodide of potassium. He had a wrist watch on, unbreakable glass, but it was under him, and it was smashed. Stopped at 2.9."

"Which is when he died?"

"Far as anybody can tell. He was out in the cold and wet for all those hours. The spray reaches that place, when the tide's high. It was going out at two, but it was still high enough to soak him. Then there was his physical condition, and nothing solid in his stomach since he had dinner at Portsmouth. Two-nine suits the medical examiner all right."

Mitchell replaced the list in the envelope, added the photograph, rose, and approached the table. He opened the lid of the pigskin dressing case, and then paused to wind a handkerchief around his right hand. A multitude of glass and silver objects winked against a rich dark-green silk lining; Gamadge came up to watch, while Mitchell began carefully to remove them one by one. They were so cunningly fitted that it was a task of some delicacy to get them out of their individual nests.

"Quite a bag," remarked Gamadge.

"How much would you say a thing like this was worth?" asked Mitchell.

"I hardly know. Where does it come from?"

Mitchell turned a flat tooth-paste container upside down, and said: "Tomlinson, Piccadilly."

"Where the good bags come from. Say five hundred dollars."

"My goodness."

"Did you see the famous cigarette case? That might have cost almost as much."

"The young feller didn't stint himself."

"He had so few toys, Mitchell. My own little car cost more than that bag, and nobody thinks it was an extravagance. He couldn't drive a car."

"You certainly liked that boy."

"I was dammed sorry for him. He must have known that it was to everybody's interest to keep him going until he was twenty-one."

"That's putting it strong. You might say, if you wanted to talk like that, that it was to his sister's interest to have him die as soon afterwards as possible."

"And to the interest of all the people benefiting by that will you're hunting for."

Mitchell took out a glittering toothbrush case. "He never even took his toothbrush. Well, that's all there is in the bag, far as I can see. Don't these things ——" He felt around the bottom edges of the lining, seized a tiny loop of ribbon, and pulled. "Not much secret about this."

"Only a compartment for valuables." Gamadge craned to look. "One pair of platinum cuff links, pearl evening studs, old-fashioned tiepin, probably his father's."

"He don't seem to have set much value on his things." Mitchell began to replace the fittings, and had just finished when somebody knocked.

"Who's there?" he demanded, hastily forcing the last objects into their places, and closing the lid.

"Sanderson."

"Come right in, Mr. Sanderson. I was waiting for you."

CHAPTER FOUR
Gamadge Assists

Sanderson came into the room like a man who has been in a hurry for so long that he cannot stop when the rush is over. The loosely hung door banged and rattled shut behind him; he crossed the room in two strides, flung himself into the chair from which Gamadge had risen, pulled out a wilting handkerchief, and dabbed his hot face with it. Gamadge retreated to the broad window ledge, where he sat in silence. Formal condolences would have been out of place; they might come later, when the young man had regained his breath and his balance. Mitchell also waited, placidly rocking.

"Hot over there at the Centre." Sanderson at last put away the handkerchief, and ran a hand over his light hair.

"Have a drink of water, Mr. Sanderson," suggested Mitchell. "You look just about all in."

"I am." He glanced about the room as if wondering how he came to be sitting there, seemed to become aware of Gamadge for the first time, and said doubtfully: "Are you—didn't I see you at the Barclay cottage last night?"

"Yes. My name's Gamadge."

"Of course. Excuse me for behaving as if I had taken leave of my senses. It was ghastly over there at the Centre this morning. The poor old Colonel had a bad time of it."

"I don't envy you the experience," said Gamadge.

"If only those two women can get through without crashing! I don't know how to face them."

"We didn't hear it was any fault of yours," said Mitchell.

"They may think it was. I never said a word to Mrs. Cowden about the boy's plan for cutting loose to-day. I hadn't the heart. He trusted me absolutely—or I thought he did." Sanderson's face expressed self-disgust. "I might have known he wouldn't have felt he could really trust anyone. He knew we were all dead against his going up there to the Cove. He simply told me enough to keep me from watching him, and made other arrangements with Atwood behind my back."

"You think he had this getaway last night all planned, then?"

"What else can I think? What was he doing down on the cliff, unless he was meeting Atwood? I suppose he was afraid that if he waited till morning I'd go on arguing, and he'd weaken, and give the whole thing up. And, of course, he could hardly wait to get there."

"But if his arrangements were all made, why did he try and get in touch with Atwood last night?"

"I'm beginning to think that he wasn't really trying to. I think that telephone call was camouflage, for my benefit. He wanted me to think that Atwood was settled up there at the Cove, and that the original plan stood for to-day. It all shows," and Sanderson gave them a wry smile, "how completely I had fallen down on my job."

"I wouldn't say that. What's your reason for this theory of yours?"

"Well, he made a call while we were at Portsmouth."

"He did?"

"Yes. He was alone in his room for a while—I thought he was asleep. It was down on the bill, but they didn't mention the destination, and like a fool I thought it was to New York. I might have noticed that the charge wasn't enough for a New York call, but we were pretty well upset and worried by that time, and I paid up and thought no more about it. He had lots of friends, you know, and all that theatre business. He liked to feel that he was in the middle of things. He was always telephoning."

"We'll check up on that call from the Harbour Inn. But see here, Mr. Sanderson; if you're right, he must have known about the telephone situation up at the Cove. Sam says he didn't know how to get through, last night. Was that camouflage, too?"

"I suppose it must have been. I'm just guessing, of course, but I can't help thinking he'd have known when and how he could get in touch with Atwood. He was very accurate, you know; he always checked up on everything. He wouldn't let any plan stand, without verification and goodness knows what all. Look here, I'm making him out a sneak."

"Sneak? No, I don't think so. We know the peculiar circumstances."

"Are you sure? He was anything but a sneak, Mitchell. And he had plenty of affection for his aunt and his sister, and a good deal for me. He simply realised what a hell of a fight I was going to put up at the last minute, and he didn't want to go through with it. He hadn't the physical strength to go through with it. You don't know how I'd been working on him. Do you know what I told him? I told him he wouldn't live a day up there. I think it was true. Just imagine," exclaimed Sanderson, almost with passion, "just imagine him living like that, or trying to! Just try to imagine him pigging it up there at that God-forsaken place. They live in tents and trailers! You can imagine how long he'd last there. It would have been the death of him. It *was* the death of him—just trying to get there," he repeated.

"Well, I suppose he realised all that, didn't he?"

"Yes, and he didn't care. He was a fearless kid, you know, which made it all the harder for us to keep him in reasonable health. He wanted a whirl before he died, and I suppose he thought the only way to get it was to go off without bother and explanation."

"I suppose if he'd gone before he was of age, Mrs. Cowden would have had him brought back?"

"He thought so, but I'm not at all sure that she would have done anything. She would have been frightfully distressed, but she wouldn't have done anything to upset him. You must remember that the one thing we all avoided was a row. His heart couldn't stand them, or so the doctors said."

"Exactly what was he going up there for, anyway?"

"To act. It isn't as crazy as it sounds; he was quite good at it. And, of course, the Atwoods flattered him. Atwood and his wife are both in that outfit, you know —'The Old Pier Players'!"

"Quite a responsibility for them, taking him up there away from his folks."

"They don't know the meaning of the word. A more irresponsible creature than Atwood never lived. All they wanted, if you ask me, was to get hold of the boy's money. The poor kid was going to be a backer, or a partner, or something."

"Sounds like a kind of skin game, to me."

"It was and it wasn't. I believe the manager, Callaghan, is a decent enough sort of person, and he really has experience in the theatre. It was a legitimate enterprise. But naturally Callaghan wants all the money he can get; he'd be glad enough to take the boy in, sick or well."

"What sort of feller is this Atwood? He must be related to a whole lot of respectable people."

"He is. His mother was Mrs. Barclay's sister. She ran off and married some sort of actor, and the family dropped her. They're both dead. Arthur Atwood is supposed to be a bad egg; I never quite made out why. He's an oddity."

"How'd young Cowden get to be so friendly with him?"

"Atwood must have engineered it. They have what they call a studio in New York—it's really nothing but a big apartment in a run-down hotel. Amby used to go there, and when I was engaged to look after him, a couple of years ago, I went along. Somebody had to look after him. But you can see how difficult the situation was; I couldn't have kept it up much longer."

"Didn't want to squeal on him—that it?"

"In the end, I simply couldn't. I should have thrown up the job, I suppose. I was losing it, anyhow, when he skipped out."

"You mean the Cowdens wouldn't have kept you on?"

"It wasn't in their hands, after he came of age. He wanted me to stay with him, but naturally I wouldn't do it; not as a member of the 'Old Pier Players'! No, I was going back to the school. I'm a schoolmaster, you know, if you can call it that. It amounts to a little lower-form teaching, mostly mathematics, sports, and general dry nursing. They've kept the job open for me. I knew, of course, that this one couldn't last long. Mrs. Cowden explained that when she took me on."

"Why'd you take such a short-term situation, anyway, Mr. Sanderson?"

"She offered me a big salary—tremendous, it seemed to me; it does still. I was to be paid for a full year, no matter what happened; as a matter of fact, I had two, and I bought myself some insurance. I went into it as a business proposition, you understand; I hadn't met Amby." He turned suddenly to Gamadge. "I suppose you didn't see enough of the boy to get any idea why I was so fond of him."

"I can easily understand your getting fond of him."

"Funny; we all knew he couldn't live long, but I got so that I stopped believing it." He got out his handkerchief again, and again dabbed his face with it. "I suppose the reason this is such a shock is because he died in that ghastly way. It's this sickening routine that makes it so bad for everybody concerned. I don't see why

Baines can't make an affidavit, or something."

"Doctor Baines wasn't attending him, was he?"

"No, I don't think he's a heart man; but he knew all about it."

"I wish you'd just give us a summary of events, up to the time you left him for good, last night."

"Starting when? The beginning of the trip? Well, he was in pretty fair shape when we left New York. We reached Boston late on Saturday, and stayed over. We planned to make Portsmouth for dinner last night; you know those shore dinners at Toms'? But he had a bad turn just before we pulled in, about seven. We stopped at this Harbour Inn, and got him to bed; tried to make him agree to spend the night there. He wouldn't hear of it; he was afraid he wouldn't get to the Old Pier in time for the opening, if he let us keep him too long on the road.

"Then there was another struggle about the Barclays. We were going to stop off there, on our way up, but we tried to persuade him to cut that out. Nothing doing; I had to telephone them that we'd be late. Late! You know what time we showed up, Gamadge. It sounds incredible, letting him do it; but I assure you, we had no choice. We were avoiding excitement; but *he* wasn't, never did.

"Well, he had another bad turn on the way up here. Not heart, so far as we could tell; just nausea and dizziness. We thought perhaps the cocoa had upset him; I suppose it was really nothing but nervousness, worrying about Atwood and the trip to the Cove. We finally drove on up, and he was as chipper as you please; the rest of us rags. He insisted on that call to the Cove, and then he turned me out. I did manage to get these things unpacked—some of them. I saw Mrs. Cowden for a minute, and asked her whether he ought to be left. She advised letting him alone. 'He'll never settle down, if you don't,' she said. You know, we were all more or less fatalists about him. It wasn't as if we could have done anything for him; there was nothing to do. So I turned in."

"And you didn't hear a thing after that?"

"I thought I heard a door closing, but like a fool I never connected the sound with him."

"I guess there wasn't any reason why you should. He doesn't seem to have taken a thing with him, Mr. Sanderson; not even his toothbrush."

"Didn't he?" Sanderson looked puzzled. "Well, he never waited on himself, you know, or carried parcels. He may actually never have thought of it. Or perhaps Atwood had things ready for him, up there, in case we retained his luggage." He laughed, sardonically. "No fear of that. Besides, you know," and he laughed again, with bitterness, "the idea was that he was going to rough it."

"Thought he could, did he?"

"I don't know what he really thought about it. He always liked to pretend that he could, if he wanted to. If we'd stuck to his original plan, I was supposed to send his stuff after him, or take it to him."

"How was he going up?"

"That's one of the things that show you what a decent kid he was; he wouldn't take the car—it's his, you know. He was going to hire one."

"Leaving you to face the music?"

"I told him I should certainly stay and face the music. That was one of the things I hoped would keep him from trying to go, at the last minute."

"You know about that will he had with him, Mr. Sanderson?"

"Yes. Colonel Barclay says it's disappeared."

"Where would you say it had got to?"

"Don't ask me, Mitchell. He was a great one for losing things."

"Still, Mr. Gamadge here says he put it in his pocket, at the Barclays'."

"He's lost plenty of things out of his pockets."

"You wouldn't say it was funny, his losing that paper?"

"I suppose it is funny. Isn't it here, in his bag, or in that dressing case? I imagined it would be found, somewhere."

"You don't seem to attach much importance to the document."

"Well, no; I don't. It wasn't signed or witnessed. Why should I attach importance to it?" Sanderson looked surprised.

"You know what was in it?"

"Oh, yes. He consulted me—or did what he called consulting me. He seldom followed my advice. He was very independent, you know."

"I'd be very glad to know what was in the thing."

"One hundred thousand dollars to Mrs. Cowden, one hundred thousand to Lieutenant Barclay, one hundred thousand to Arthur Atwood, a thousand to me, and the rest to his sister."

"My goodness, he was no piker!"

"No; he wasn't. I thought it a very good will, except for the Atwood bequest; but that," and Sanderson gave a wry smile, "was supposed to be dedicated to the interests of the drama."

"Oh. Atwood was to administer it, was he?"

"I made a feeble attempt to get it put into some form of trust."

"This Atwood must have had him hypnotised."

"Sometimes I thought it almost amounted to that."

"He didn't leave you much, Mr. Sanderson."

"I thought it a generous legacy, considering that he had only known me a couple of years, and that I spent my life bedeviling him, poor kid."

Gamadge spoke from the void. "Have you looked in the car?"

"What say?" enquired Mitchell, turning sharply to look at him.

"That document; couldn't it have been dropped in the car—on the way up here from the Barclay cottage? He was sick; there must have been more or less fuss and bother; mightn't it have been lost then?"

"I never thought of that." Sanderson considered it. "Possible."

Mitchell was already at the telephone. He pulled it over to him without leaving his chair, and spoke to the office: "I want the garage." After a moment he said: "Garage? This is the police. You know the Cowden car? Anybody been near it since it came in last night?...How do you know? Where's the night man?...Told you not a soul came near the place after it got in? Well, Mr. Sanderson will be down with the keys. He'll lock it up. I'm coming down later, and I'll go over it. Keep an eye on it. Thanks."

He put up the receiver. Sanderson rose. "I'll have a word with the Colonel," he said. "He wants me to go over to the Centre with him again before lunch. I offered to drive him, but we'll have to use his car again—if it lasts the trip."

"Just one minute more, Mr. Sanderson." Mitchell caught his eye, and held it. "Would you mind telling me what you think happened down there on that cliff?"

Sanderson's face changed, and hardened. He said without hesitation: "I would mind, Mitchell; I have no ideas on the subject, and if I had, they wouldn't be worth listening to. I can't imagine what happened."

"You can imagine his going down there, and having a fatal heart attack, the one you were all expecting at any minute, day and night, and falling off that rock—can't you?"

"Yes. No doubt that is what happened."

"You think Atwood drove down there——"

"I don't even know whether Atwood got a message, asking him to come."

"Say he did, and drove down. He might have gone up to the top of the cliff, and waited, and then gone back again, thinking the boy hadn't been able to make it."

"He might."

"Wouldn't see the body, perhaps, in all that fog."

"Quite likely."

"You know the feller; if he had seen it, would he be the kind to go on back to the Cove without doing anything about it?"

"That's what I don't care to theorise about. I have no particular liking for Atwood; but I have no right to make wild guesses as to what he might or mightn't do. It would be absurd."

"I'm not asking you to gossip, Mr. Sanderson; I merely want your opinion, based on what you know of the feller's character."

"He's a complete enigma to me."

"You said he was irresponsible."

"He always seemed so, to me. How far it goes, I can't say."

"Well, thanks. I guess that's all."

When he had gone, Mitchell observed, in a dissatisfied tone: "I wish I had some kind of a line on all these people; nobody knows 'em, up here. But that kind of enquiry takes time."

"How about letting me telephone my assistant? He's good at that sort of thing, and he'd do the routine stuff without publicity."

"What does he assist you at?"

"He helps me to analyse paper, ink, glue, handwriting, print, and other things connected with books and manuscripts."

"And looks up people for you?"

"And takes care of the cat. And helps Theodore around the house."

"Who's Theodore?" Mitchell was amused.

"Old coloured man that takes care of me. I live in an old house in the Sixties

—where I was born, as a matter of fact; but I've turned half of it into workshops, now."

"What is this business of yours, Mr. Gamadge?"

"It has no name. But if somebody wants to sell you a rare old pamphlet about Nell Gwyn, with Charles the Second's autograph on the flyleaf and marginal notes by Louis the Fourteenth, I'll perhaps be able to tell you whether it was made later than 1900, and what part of Michigan it came from."

"You make a living that way, Mr. Gamadge?"

"That's telling. People pay me for doing it, though."

"I don't know about telephoning; especially through this exchange."

"Oh, Harold and I have a code." Gamadge fished a little green book out of his pocket, and ruffled the pages with an air of resignation.

"Code, have you?" Mitchell watched him, very much tickled.

"Yes. He made it up. He's very young, you know, and he likes to imagine that our occupation is romantic and risky. Perhaps he thinks that some maddened forger of colophons will get after us. Trouble is, whenever I use the thing—which is about once a year—I feel like a fool."

"Pick that receiver up the way I did."

"Right you are."

Gamadge asked for Long Distance, and then gave a number.

"Where'd you get hold of this Harold?" enquired Mitchell, while they waited.

"He got hold of me…That you, Harold? How are you? How's Theodore? How's Martin? Off his feed, is he? Of course he's off his feed. Never let anybody tell you cats have no feelings. He's moping for me. What's that? Something he *ate*? If it's something he ate, you're fired, and I'll have Theodore's life.

"Have you got your little green book there? Good. I want you to take down some names; friends of mine up here that have had a bereavement. Young man killed—you'll see about it in the papers. These relations of his will all be back in New York tomorrow or next day, and I want you to get in touch with them, and offer your services. Look up the addresses, you know. Here are the names: Mrs. Francis Cowden, Miss Alma Cowden (that's her niece), Colonel Harrison Barclay, his wife, and his son Frederic; and a Mr. Hugh Sanderson, the tutor of the boy who was killed. Got all that? All right. Er—Potto." He hung up.

"What's 'Potto'?" enquired Mitchell, laughing.

"Don't ask me what it is. Harold says it's a South American animal. It means: 'Full information required on the foregoing'—or at least, I hope it does."

"How will he get the information?"

"Don't ask me that, either; but if it's to be had, he'll have it."

They went out into the hall, and Mitchell, after locking the door, sealed it with several strips of gummed paper. "They tell me nobody came in here since last night," he said, "but I might as well get the place printed."

"Who tells you?"

"Colonel Barclay. He telephoned up to the hotel for me, and found out. That the fire escape, out there?"

"Yes. The only wooden one now in existence. It's stronger than it looks."

They went out on the platform, and Mitchell looked up, and then down. A narrow spiral stairway encircled the open shaft of the freight elevator, its only guard a single rail.

"I wouldn't want to use this myself, not on a foggy night," said Mitchell. He glanced out at the peaceful view before him; cottages and ocean to the right, pines to the north, rolling golf course to the west. Immediately in front was the garage, and beyond it was the little clubhouse, its flag waving gently in the land breeze. A voice from the corridor made him turn. It said: "Good morning, Mr. Gamadge. Will you introduce me to the detective?"

CHAPTER FIVE
Terror by Daylight

Mrs. Barclay, wearing a pink woollen coat and skirt, white beach shoes, and a large white felt hat, stood outside the door of Room 21, clutching a knitting bag to her breast. The two men stepped into the corridor, and Gamadge performed introductions.

"You want to see me, ma'am?" asked Mitchell.

"Yes, I do."

"That's good. It saves me a trip to your cottage." He tried the door of Number 22, which opened. "Step in here, Mrs. Barclay. It don't seem to be occupied."

"You too, if you'll be so good, Mr. Gamadge," said Mrs. Barclay. Her eyes were red, but her expression showed less grief than anger and determination. She walked in, followed by the others. Gamadge closed the door.

"Dreadful thing, Mr. Gamadge, isn't it?" Mrs. Barclay sat down on the edge of the bed, her beach shoes close together. "I have been trying to see my niece, but Eleanor tells me she is prostrated. I brought a tonic for her. My sister-in-law does not seem to feel that she would be the better for it."

"I think they had Baines," said Gamadge.

"Who will give her the inevitable sedative, and depress her still further. What do you make of this terrible affair, Mr. Mitchell?"

"That's what I was going to ask you, ma'am."

"Not one of us knows what to think. My son, who was as intimate with Amberley as anybody, simply cannot imagine what got into him. It was bad enough for him to be planning to go at all; but for him to creep off like that, in the middle of the night, without a word to anyone! And after all my sister-in-law had done for him! Of course, Mr. Mitchell, my nephew Amberley was very much spoiled. They gave way to him in everything."

"That so, ma'am?"

"It wasn't only that he was an invalid; he was also very generous to them. Not that my sister-in-law had no money of her own; far from it. My brother left her comfortably provided for. Her income is not what it was, but she is independent."

"That's good."

"She has always supported my niece Alma, who has nothing, poor child; or practically nothing."

"Had, Mrs. Barclay," said Mitchell. "I understand she has plenty, now."

"Oh—yes. Do you know," and Mrs. Barclay smiled at him, "I keep forgetting! We are so used to thinking of the child as nearly penniless. Which brings me to what I wanted to say to you. You know about that will of my nephew's, Mr. Mitchell?"

"Yes, I heard about it."

"You know it is lost?"

"We haven't found it, yet."

"Mr. Mitchell, that will must be found! No stone must be left unturned. Have you a search warrant?"

"Well, no. I didn't expect to need one."

"You do indeed need one."

"Who would you like me to search, ma'am?"

"Everybody, and every room they occupy! It is a serious matter, Mr. Mitchell. Do you know what was in that will?"

"Yes, I heard what was in it."

"I make no accusations; I insinuate nothing. I am willing to believe that it has been mislaid; but I insist that every effort be made to find it. Mr. Gamadge saw it, in our cottage, and he saw it replaced in Amberley's pocket; so much for *us*. We are out of it; and, moreover, nobody has a stronger motive than ours for wanting it found."

"Except this Atwood."

Mrs. Barclay winced. "Which makes it all the more absurd," she went on, recovering herself, "to think that *he* is sequestering it."

"Let me get this clear, Mrs. Barclay. Is it your idea that Miss Cowden is sequestering it? She's the only person I know of that has any motive for doing such a thing."

"I said, Mr. Mitchell, that I accuse no one, and I insinuate nothing. All I say is, that will must not be allowed to disappear without a search being made for it. A search by experts. Do you realise that the bequests in it amount to more than three hundred thousand dollars?"

"Well, yes, Mrs. Barclay; but the thing wasn't signed or witnessed, you know."

"I have been told, on good authority, that in some cases, and under certain conditions, the bequests in a holograph will are upheld by the courts, even if that will is not signed or witnessed."

"You may be right, ma'am. I'm no lawyer. We're looking for it."

"I am not a beneficiary, but I shall gladly pay an investigator; payment to depend on finding and proving the will, of course."

"You might find somebody to do it for you on those terms."

"Or I might offer a contingent reward."

"I'll tell you something, ma'am; we haven't done looking, yet; but if we don't find it, you can be pretty sure it won't be found. It don't take long to destroy a piece of paper, and if anybody took it, they'd destroy it. That's the only reason they would take it."

"Then," said Mrs. Barclay, compressing her lips, "I shall make trouble."

"Watch your step, ma'am. That's dangerous. The kind of trouble you mean involves talk, doesn't it?"

"Talk to the proper authorities isn't slander, Mr. Mitchell."

"But the proper authorities know all there is to know now, don't they? Or don't they?" asked Mitchell, hopefully. "You got any information about last night, Mrs. Barclay?"

"I know nothing about what happened last night."

"So the Colonel said."

"What should we know about it? We were all in bed fifteen or twenty minutes after the Cowdens left, soon after half-past twelve. We stacked the glasses, and we went to bed."

"You know of your own knowledge that the Colonel and Mr. Barclay went to bed?"

"Of course I know it. What else should they do?"

"But the Colonel says you all have separate rooms, and sleep with the doors shut."

"We do, of course. The draughts in our cottage are dreadful; and Fred says his father snores."

"You have no maid?"

"Not here, Mr. Mitchell. We camp, at the beach. It makes us so much more independent. I fail to see why you are asking me these questions."

"You talked as if you had some inside information, ma'am."

"My information lies in the realm of psychology, Mr. Mitchell. Alma Cowden is completely under the influence of her aunt; she will not be permitted to carry out her brother's wishes. If enough publicity is given to the loss of that will, they may be forced, in self-defence, to do the proper thing. That is all I meant."

"Just watch your step; you might run into something tough, there."

There was a sharp knock at the door, and Fred Barclay came in without waiting to be invited. He cast a long, slow look about the room, and said: "Hello, Gamadge. On the carpet? He's an innocent bystander, Mitchell."

A subtle change had come over Lieutenant Barclay since the preceding night. Gamadge could not make out where it lay, or exactly how it manifested itself; the young man's impassivity was as it had always been, his ironical air the same, his calm drawl unaltered; but Gamadge wondered whether all this façade, instead of being a sort of second nature, were not now, for the first time, deliberately assumed and used to hide something. There was a lack of spontaneity somewhere.

"Telling all, Mum?" continued Barclay. "Dad *will* be pleased. You know you promised——"

"Freddy, I cannot help it! With your whole future at stake——"

"You be careful. You know Aunt El isn't the woman to stand that sort of thing. Pay no attention to Mother, you two; she's had a disappointment. Or that's rather a mild way of putting it. A blow—a staggering blow. So have one or two others. And that's what money does to the human animal; it isn't poor old Amby we're shedding tears over this morning."

"Freddy!" Mrs. Barclay's eyes began to water. "You know very well——"

"I know. Never mind. Have you seen Alma?"

"No. Eleanor wouldn't let me."

"*Incommunicado*, is she?"

"I do wish she would take some of Aunt Julia's tonic. It always soothes the nerves, and there is no harmful reaction."

"You and your tonic." Mr. Barclay took his mother's arm and helped her up, not unkindly. "You come on down to the beach, or back home, before you get us all in a jam. Forget it."

He nodded to the others, and escorted Mrs. Barclay firmly from the room. After a pause Gamadge remarked: "I should have said there was nothing terrifying about Mrs. Barclay but her opening four bid at bridge."

"She's loony about that boy of hers," said Mitchell.

He led the way across the hall, and knocked at the door of Room 21. A quiet voice told them to come in.

Mrs. Cowden sat beside the north window of a large, square room, which was pleasantly furnished with flowery chintz and green wicker. There was a pen in her hand, and a pile of telegraph forms in front of her; she wore a plain white blouse and skirt; and white shoes. Her reading glasses changed her very much. They, and her pallor, had aged her by ten years.

She took them off, and got up. "Is this Mr. Mitchell?" she asked.

"Yes, Mrs. Cowden. I wouldn't have thought of bothering you to-day, only Mr. Gamadge——"

"He was quite right. It isn't for me to collapse. There is too much to do, and Alma to be taken care of. You were very kind to offer to help, Mr. Gamadge. Won't you both sit down?"

They did so, and Mitchell got out a notebook. "I just want some statistics," he said.

"For the inquest?"

"Well, yes, ma'am. Then you won't have to attend."

"I'll go if necessary."

"Colonel Barclay will do that. You were the guardian of this young man, Mrs. Cowden?"

"Yes, and his sister's. My husband was appointed under their father's will, and when he died the court appointed me."

"Miss Cowden is her brother's heir, I understand."

"Yes. They have no blood relations except their aunt, Mrs. Barclay, and Fred Barclay, and Arthur Atwood. He's another cousin."

"I've heard of him. How old is the young lady?"

"Nineteen."

"Who's going to administer her estate for her?"

"I have no idea. I have asked Mr. Ormville, our lawyer, to come up; he'll be here in the morning, and he'll tell you all about it."

"We know how you must feel about all this, Mrs. Cowden, and the sheriff don't want you to have any more trouble than we can help. It was a natural death, far as we can tell, only when the newspapers get hold of it, they'll say the circumstances were mysterious. You know how they go on. So if we could find out why your nephew went down there to that rock, it would cut your publicity down to about one-fiftieth."

"I know, Mr. Mitchell. Unfortunately, to me and to all the rest of us here the circumstances *are* mysterious. We cannot imagine why he went down there, unless it was to meet his cousin Arthur. I didn't even know that he meant to leave us to-day. Poor Hugh Sanderson gave me my first news of that this morning. Of course I knew that he wanted to go off somewhere, as soon as he came of age; but I hoped he would give it up, or take a short trip with Mr. Sanderson."

The communicating door was flung open, and Alma Cowden dashed into the room. She wore a white linen dress, much crumpled, and she held out a little package. She said, violently: "I won't take this stuff, Aunt Eleanor. I won't do it."

Mrs. Cowden addressed her niece mildly. "You remember Mr. Gamadge, Alma? And this is State Detective Mitchell."

Miss Cowden checked, nodded shortly, and repeated; "I won't take this and go to sleep. I want to get out of here."

Her eyelids were swollen, her face flushed, and her dark eyes wild and glazed like those of a frightened colt. Her aunt said: "You can go for a drive, my dearest child, as soon as Hugh Sanderson has time to take you."

"I can't stay in that room a minute longer."

"You could, if you would just take——"

"I want to go for a walk by myself."

"You simply can't wander about alone to-day."

"There might be newspaper fellers around, photographers, all kinds of people," said Mitchell, sympathetically.

"Please do what Doctor Baines ordered." Mrs. Cowden, in spite of her iron control, was visibly at the end of her tether. The girl gazed about her as if in desperation, then went over to the east window and stood with her back to the room. Gamadge sat watching her, and then, while Mitchell's benevolent voice continued to ask questions, which were followed by Mrs. Cowden's prompt, taut replies, he got up and lurched across. She did not move when he propped himself against the window seat. After a moment he asked: "Why don't you bite on it?"

She flashed a look on him, and looked away.

"When a thing like this happens," he went on, "it's bad for everybody. Nothing's finer than being a sheltered member of the community, with friends among the traffic cops, and everybody falling over themselves to keep you comfortable, and the law—even in a little place like this—shooting around looking after you. But it's an awfully poor preparation for you, if things don't go right, and you have to pay the price."

She glanced at him again, looked away, and looked back. "Price?"

"The price of living in a civilised world," he said. "If, through no fault of your own, you get involved in these complicated machines we have set going to keep us going, you have to become a well-oiled cog, or you get smashed. Now you're trying to behave and feel as if nothing had happened, except a personal bereavement. Why? You don't look stupid to me, and you don't look like an egomaniac. All that's asked of you is to take some dope and go to sleep. Why don't you do it?"

She said: "I'm afraid of sleeping stuff."

"No, you're not. But you look to me as if you were afraid of something else."

"What do you say that for? I'm all right." She stared at him, sideways; the whites of her eyes showed, more coltishly than ever.

"No, you're not. Look here, Baines knows his business. He wouldn't have sent you that stuff for fun. Why don't you take it? Take your medicine, as the phrase goes?" As she made no answer, he went on, so low that the others could not hear what he said: "What's scared you half out of your wits?"

"Nothing."

"Don't tell me that. You're so scared you think you'd better keep your wits about you. That's why you won't take sleeping stuff." He added, "I won't tell anybody."

She said, in a muffled voice: "That will Amby was going to sign."

"Yes; what about it?"

"I'm going to pay all those legacies, when I get the money."

"Very nice of you. When do you get it?"

"I don't know. Shall I have to wait two years—till I'm of age?"

"I should think so."

"But I could let everybody know I was going to pay them the money."

"You could. They'll probably give you the income your brother had, until you get the capital. If you wanted to, I suppose you could begin paying the beneficiaries out of that." He looked at her pallid face, and said: "Let me get this straight; are you afraid that somebody's going to get impatient, and do you in?"

"No; of course not."

He disregarded her faint denial, and went on: "What does your aunt think of the idea, or haven't you told her about it?"

"She thinks it's ridiculous."

"Well; let's see. Sanderson's out, I should think—you'll have to stay alive, if he's to get his thousand dollars. Besides, you can easily pay *him* off."

"Laugh at me, if you want to; the way my aunt does."

"I was never less amused in my life. Sanderson being eliminated, things begin to narrow down a little. What's this cousin of yours really like—this Atwood? Do you know him?"

Miss Cowden's shoulders moved, almost as if she shuddered. "Yes, I know him. He's awful."

"Awful, is he? Your brother thought a lot of him."

"Amby liked all sorts of people, if they made him have a good time."

"I'm going up to the Cove. Do you want me to let this hobgoblin know that you're going to give him his hundred thousand?"

"Yes."

"And shall I tell the Barclays?"

"Aunt Eleanor's going to tell the Barclays."

"I wouldn't be too sure about that, if she hears how Mrs. Barclay has been going on." Alma Cowden's trembling lip curled. Gamadge continued: "Now, listen, Miss Cowden; I don't quite know what to think of this dismal idea of yours; it may be the result of shock. You've had a terrific shock, you know. No use people saying you must have been prepared; nobody is ever prepared. Nothing can prepare you."

She glanced at him, as if surprised that he should realise this fact.

"I don't know these people," he went on, "and I can't even guess whether your feeling is justified; but I do know a blue funk when I see one. There's no reason why you should be left to get out of it as best you can. I'll fix things for you."

"Nobody can fix them."

"That's what you think. It's easy. What's that dope you have there?"

"Luminal."

"That's the stuff! Pay attention, now; I'll have Mitchell post a man in Room 22; to keep the newspaper men off, you understand? He won't let anybody come near you, not even a member of the family. I'll put a sign on the door that you're not to be disturbed. Now comes the expert advice from a past master on the heebie-jeebies: Take one of those tablets, and get into a tepid bath. Stay in it for twenty minutes, no more, no less. By the time you're out, of it, the man will be on guard—I'll knock when he is, and tell you so. Lock both doors; somebody might barge in through your aunt's room with lunch, or something, and I want you to feel that you're not going to be waked. Get into bed, and take the second tablet; by that time your room will be nice and shady—you'll be asleep in five minutes. How does that sound?"

The shadow of a smile touched Miss Cowden's lips. "It sounds nice."

"You'll sleep right through lunch. Have you anything to amuse yourself with, when you do wake up?"

"I'm knitting a sweater."

"Good. Telephone down and order yourself something or other—a glass of milk, tea and toast, something light. You won't want much, but you ought to have something. After you get it, stay right in your room and knit until I get back from Seal Cove. When I do, we're going out for a turn on the golf course."

"Aunt El won't let me do that."

"She will, when I've talked to her. It's the best time of day for a walk; cool, pleasant, and hardly anybody playing. You needn't play, you know; just take a club and help me look for balls. Will you start now on the Gamadge Hydropathic Treatment? I want to hear the bath running before I go, and your aunt and Mitchell look as if they'd finished their conference."

"Yes, I will."

Miss Cowden left the room so quietly that neither Mitchell nor Mrs. Cowden looked around. When Gamadge joined them, she was saying: "…cannot imagine where it is. Perhaps he did drop it in the car. Alma is very anxious to carry out the bequests, so the will is of no importance, in any case."

"Just in case somebody got to talking, we might as well have a try at finding it," said Mitchell. "I'll take a witness and go over the car, do it formal."

"There's no hurry, we shan't be using it."

"Well, I'm much obliged to you. I guess that's all."

Mrs. Cowden shifted telegraph forms about on the table. She said: "I hope I haven't seemed abrupt. I'm not quite myself."

"I think you've been fine."

"It's this ghastly feeling that I've failed at my job."

"Don't feel that way."

"I completely lost his confidence when I interfered about the Atwoods."

"I don't believe any older person ever does have a young one's full confidence. Your nephew never had much of a chance at a private life, I guess. I ain't surprised, myself, that he wanted to have a try for one. You had quite a problem on your hands."

Gamadge asked: "Has Mitchell told you that he's putting a man in Room 22, to keep you from being annoyed in any way?"

"No; what a splendid idea!"

Gamadge hurried on, to cover Mitchell's wooden stare: "I've persuaded your niece to take her sleeping medicine."

Mrs. Cowden said, with the ghost of a smile: "Young men have so much more influence with young women than aunts and doctors seem to have."

"She looks upon me as an old uncle. Look here, Mrs. Cowden; she was right, you know. What you both need is a walk. How about a stroll on the golf course, late this afternoon? Now don't say no; I can arrange it so you won't see anybody, and nobody will see you. You can go down the fire escape, and along that path behind the club-house to the tenth tee. The second nine is all among woods, and what few golfers there are will all be in by that time."

Mrs. Cowden looked doubtful, thought a moment, and said at last that she might consider it. "It's most kind of you, Mr. Gamadge. It's an imposition. What about your own golf?"

"I have no match on to-day. Why not let me make myself useful? I'll send one of the boys up when we get back from Seal Cove."

"Are you going up there?"

"I'm driving Mitchell up. I thought if you could spare him we might take Sanderson along; he knows Atwood."

"Of course I can spare him; but I don't believe poor Hugh Sanderson is likely to get any information out of Arthur Atwood. I don't think anybody could."

"I'm really getting very curious to meet the fellow. Until later, then."

He got himself out of the room, across the hall, and to the telephone in Room 22 before Mitchell had managed to make his farewells. He had, indeed, got his connection with the garage, and ordered his car to be sent up to the hotel, before Mitchell advanced upon him:

"Who arranged about me being the stooge around here?"

"Now, wait a minute; those women are in a state. They need privacy. I thought you'd approve of my suggestion about posting a man here."

"You're mighty considerate of them, all of a sudden. Mrs. Cowden—she's as nice a lady as I ever met. She had no more to do with her nephew's death than I had."

"Sold on Mrs. Cowden; I knew you'd like her."

"She's feeling terrible, but she can hold it in. That girl can't. I never saw anybody worse overwrought."

"I wondered what you'd think of Miss Cowden."

"You were talking to her; what do you think of her?"

"She is spirited—very spirited."

"Too spirited to suit me. I like her aunt's way of being spirited better."

"It's admirable. But I have a feeling that without money, Mrs. Cowden as we know her would cease to exist. Can you dig up somebody to look after these women, or must I do it myself?"

"Call the office, if you don't mind, and have them send up a boy."

Gamadge did so, explaining: "Yes, this is 22, Wilks; Mitchell and I are conferring in it. And if Mr. Sanderson comes in, ask him to speak to us, will you?"

Waldo arrived, panting, and Mitchell said: "You won't last the season out, at this rate, young feller. Take those stairs easy, or you'll founder yourself. College boy, ain't you?"

"Yes, sir."

"What's your last name? Ames, is it? Your father Doctor Waldo Ames, Oakport?"

"Yes, he is, Mr. Mitchell."

"Then you ought to be a responsible kind of feller, if you're anything like him. I want you to go down and give Parker a confidential message from me. Ask him if we can use this room to-day on sheriff's business."

"Yes, Mr. Mitchell."

"That deputy, Hoskins. He still downstairs?"

"Yes, he's on the front steps."

"Bring him up here with you."

Waldo sped off. Mitchell remarked: "Boy comes of good stock."

"I like Peabody the best," murmured Gamadge.

They sat with the door open, until a small, wiry man in shirtsleeves, his coat over his arm, came in at a leisurely pace. Mitchell said: "Hoskins, this is Mr. Gamadge. He wants you to do something, and he'd better tell you what it is. I think he wants you to act as a kind of bouncer. Too bad you ain't a bigger man, but you're the best I can do."

Gamadge ignored this. "I'll tell you how it is, Hoskins," he said. "These ladies in 21 and 19—Mrs. Cowden and Miss Cowden, you know—they're badly shaken up, nervous, suffering from shock, all that kind of thing. I don't want any stranger to go near them. You're to do any knocking on Mrs. Cowden's door that has to be done, and you'll deliver any or all messages. And nobody, I don't care who, is to disturb Miss Cowden for any reason. She's resting by doctor's orders. I'm going to put a sign up. If she wants anything, she'll tell you."

Hoskins asked: "When do I eat?"

"Whenever you want to. Telephone down, and ask them to put the bill on my account. But we don't want to be too conspicuous; the other guests might not like it."

"How would it be if I borrowed one of the porters' uniforms?"

"Great idea; you have your wits about you. Now, if you'll come across the hall with me, I'll introduce you to Miss Cowden."

Gamadge's tap on the door of Room 19 brought a faint response: "Who is it?"

"Me; Gamadge. I want to introduce Mr. Deputy Sheriff Hoskins."

"How do?" said Hoskins, to the pine surface in front of him.

"How do you do?" came through the door.

"He's the nicest little man you ever met, Miss Cowden, and he has absolutely caught the spirit of the occasion. He has suggested wearing a porter's uniform, so that it won't look funny for him to hang around watching the fire escape. I'll describe him for you: red hair, red face, light-blue eyes set rather close together, but not disagreeably so; longish nose, biggish ears, biggish mouth, no collar."

"I'd know him anywhere," said the voice on the other side of the door.

"Very well, then; it's thoroughly understood that if you feel at all nervous, and don't care about ringing down and telling the office about it, and don't wish to knock up your aunt and have her tell you that it's all imagination, you're to bang on your door, or open it and call out. Hoskins will come running. If anybody has any business with you from now on until I get back, they'll have to transact it through Hoskins. I'm off to the Cove, with Mitchell and Sanderson. When I get back, you and I and your aunt are going to have that golf game. How do you feel? Sleepy?"

"Yes, I do. Thank you."

"Till later, then."

Gamadge took an envelope out of his pocket, wrote: "Asleep. Do Not Disturb" on it, and handed it to Hoskins. "Get one of the boys to give you a thumbtack," he said, "and put this under the number on the door."

CHAPTER SIX
The Pottery Pig

Mitchell came out of Room 22. "Oakport tells me that a tea room called the 'Pottery Pig' is taking messages for the Cove," he said, as he and Gamadge went down the corridor. "We might as well stop there and see whether they got any telephone call yesterday from the Harbour Inn. I suppose they write the messages down. I don't make a practice of expecting too much, but that message, if we get hold of it, might just settle the whole thing."

"You didn't call the Harbour Inn?"

"May not need to. Besides, they might not have listened in on the talk, and it would have been the night shift, anyway, I guess. This place is our best bet."

"If we like the look of it, we can lunch there."

Sanderson was at the lobby desk, sorting mail. He said he would be very glad to go up to the Cove with them, if Mrs. Cowden could spare him. "She says she can? Then I'll send these up, and get the car."

"Mine is at the door," said Gamadge, "if one of you doesn't object to the rumble. It isn't bad."

"I don't object to it in the least. Here, Waldo."

"Tell him not to get mad at the sentry. Little Hoskins, the deputy, is on guard up there."

"He is? What for?"

"We don't want the ladies annoyed by anybody. You don't get much protection in a little place like this, with no floor clerks or elevators," explained Mitchell.

"That's true. What a good idea!"

Mitchell accepted the compliment with dignity, ignoring Gamadge's wink and the reproachful comment of Wilks, the day clerk: "We wouldn't let anybody up, Mr. Mitchell."

"There's the fire escape, Wilks," Gamadge reminded him.

"We could lock it, and take away the key."

"Don't tell Mitchell that, or he'll tell the fire chief."

Waldo was dispatched upstairs with the letters, and the three went out on the veranda. Gamadge paused before a poster tacked up on the bulletin board outside the door:

Monday, June 26, to Saturday, *July 1*

at 8.45 p.m.

THE OLD PIER PLAYERS

of

Seal Cove, Maine

in

THREE CELEBRATED PLAYS

"Well," he said, "perhaps they're right to work up the suspense. I can think of one or two celebrated plays I wouldn't go to see; not if you paid me."

Mitchell grumbled, "I don't know what possessed those people to pick on the Cove! I shouldn't think even summer folks would want to slosh up there, 'specially on a bad night."

"Was it always a theatre?" asked Sanderson.

"No; it was a fish-house. Then some carnival people fixed it up, but they quit after a season or two. It's been pretty much of a ruin these last few years, till this Callaghan came along. I'll be surprised if he finds his troupe can eat off it."

"Don't forget that Callaghan expected a backer," Sanderson reminded him, grimly.

"I guess Callaghan didn't know how much of a gamble it was."

Gamadge's coupé had been parked near the front steps. He opened the rumble, and folded back the convertible top; the others meanwhile tossing for seats. It ended by Mitchell clambering cheerfully up into the rear, while the others slid into the front of the car.

"And you're lucky not to be taking anything bigger than this up there," Mitchell assured them, gloomily. "That lane from Tucon to the Cove, you couldn't pass a breakdown in it; or turn, either. You'd have to wait for the wreckers. Turn down to the cliff, first, if you don't mind, Mr. Gamadge. I want to speak to the man I left there."

Gamadge drove to the end of the Ocean House drive, and then obeyed instructions. He stopped twenty yards farther on, where a sandy track led upwards between rocks. A state policeman's head rose above the sky line.

"What's he doing there?" asked Gamadge.

"He was keeping the road clear; there was quite a jam this morning." Mitchell climbed down. "You coming up?"

Gamadge said he was, and slid from beneath the wheel; Sanderson shook his head.

"I was there this morning. I'll wait here, thanks." He lighted a cigarette, while Mitchell went up the path, and Gamadge stood glancing about him.

Across the road lay the hotel precincts, which comprised two or three acres of rough land, thickly overgrown and practically in a state of nature. The roofs of several shingled cottages barely showed through the jungle. On the seaward side, the cliffs ended abruptly not far beyond the "Lookout"; they formed one boundary of the bathing beach, which was separated from the highway by a sea wall. The road here broadened into a wide loop, and disappeared around a sharp bend. There was a lamp post at the loop, and another at the entrance to the Ocean House. Gamadge said: "Pretty dark here, last night. I remember what it was like. He must have had a torch even to see the track."

"The white sand shows up, almost like snow." Sanderson glanced at the track to the "Lookout." "Still, it seems incredible that he should have gone up there…alone."

"I suppose that bench up there is a good place to watch for a car. Nobody wants to stand in the road on a foggy night, with that hairpin kind of bend on one side of him, and cars shooting over the crest of a hill on the other. And this pedestrian couldn't jump for it."

"He had a little flashlight—very nice one; all his things were the last word. Perhaps he had it with him, but I didn't see it."

Gamadge climbed the short, easy ascent to a small plateau. It was wide for its length—about eight feet by ten—and carpeted deeply with trampled sand. The bench, a sturdy wooden affair, had long since lost all its paint, and was carved from back to legs with initials and romantic symbols. Mitchell and the young officer stepped aside, and Gamadge went to the brink of the cliff and looked down.

It was a sheer drop of thirty feet, with waterworn reddish stone below. Sharper rocks, enclosing shallow pools, went down in rough terraces to the narrow strip of beach, which diminished with every incoming wave. A small crowd stood on the sand, retreating from the lines of surf, but still gazing obstinately upward.

"Tide's driven most of 'em off," said the trooper.

"The body lay just there." Mitchell pointed to the smooth rock above the pool. "It was wet through."

"I'm going down." Gamadge followed the cliff for a few yards, and then descended by a narrow crevasse, damp and, finally, barnacled. He circled the foot of the rocks, and climbed up to the spot above the pool. Here he stood, hands in pockets, shoulders a little hunched, and viewed the scene; glanced at the bathing beach to his right, which was blooming with brightly-coloured umbrellas; studied the pool at his feet, the sand below, and the towering walls above. At last he returned to the beach, and came back to the road in a leisurely fashion, via the boardwalk.

Mitchell and the state policeman met him at the car.

"You go and get your dinner, Pottle," said the former. "No reason for you to stay up there any longer. I'm going to Seal Cove, and I don't know how long I'll be, but I want to get back here by four, to meet the fingerprint man from Portland. You hang around up at the Ocean House and hang on to him for me."

He and Gamadge got into the car. Gamadge drove down to the loop, turned there, and headed back up the hill.

They passed the Ocean House and its grounds, dipped to sea level, and followed the shore for a mile and a half. The road then swerved left, and ran between pines to Oakport Village, somnolent beside the wharves where canoes and sailboats bobbed on dark waters. They left the village behind, and turned out of a stately avenue of elms to a by-road whose sign said: "Tucon, 3 miles. Seal Cove, 3½ miles."

"You can come by the state road," said Mitchell, "but it's a couple of miles longer. They don't seem to have got around to mending this one."

Gamadge steered around an outcropping rock, ploughed into the ditch, and ploughed out again, blackberry vines in flower swishing against the wheels.

"No, you're right, they don't," he agreed, wrenching at the wheel. They were already in the deep country; daisy fields and stony pastures to right and left, elms and oaks rising against a clear blue sky.

"And I suppose this was the trip Amberley was proposing to make, at night, in a fog," muttered Sanderson. "He wouldn't have got there alive. Gamadge, have you seen Miss Cowden?"

"Yes. She came in for a minute or two, while Mitchell was talking to her aunt. I got Mrs. Cowden to see him, you know."

"I didn't. How is she taking it, Gamadge? Is she badly knocked up?"

"About what you'd expect."

"I don't know what I expect. I expect her to take it pretty hard."

"She is taking it hard."

"She and Amberley thought a lot of each other. She's a clever girl—has brains. If only I'd come along earlier, I think I might have done something about it—got her to a first-rate school; college; wangled something or other for her. Amberley didn't realise—he was too young, too much handicapped by his struggle to stay alive. Mrs. Cowden never liked to ask him for money—he did so many other things for them. He was just beginning to understand the situation. Oh, well; she'll be all right, now."

"How'd you come to get the job?" asked Mitchell.

"I met Mrs. Cowden at a friend's country house. Her people had known mine, and she was kind enough to be interested. I was teaching at the Hillburn school. She thought he'd like me; and so he did. It's a good deal of a blow to find out how fed up he was getting with us all."

"I still think it's funny he didn't leave you more in that will."

Sanderson half turned, and looked up at Mitchell. "It sounds phony, I know, but I wouldn't let him. You might understand, if you knew all the circumstances."

"Any objection to telling some of 'em?"

"No particular objection. My family had money, once; but ever since I was old enough to notice, we've been poor relations. When I was under seventeen, I swore I'd get out of that situation, or die in the attempt; and that I'd never get back into it again as long as I lived. Well, I've managed to support myself since then, and I've been independent. I don't mind living plainly. When I got into the Cowden family, I saw the whole thing over again—a bunch of people living on that boy's expectations. I made up my mind that he wouldn't be able to think of me like that; I wanted him to feel that there was one person in the world who didn't care whether he ever came into money or not. Sounds pretty sanctimonious, doesn't it?"

Gamadge glanced at his flushed face. "You're sunk," he said. "Did you get any breakfast?"

"The Colonel and I had coffee at a hot-dog stand."

"I'm standing the party lunch at the 'Pottery Pig.' You'll feel better when you've had something to eat. When a thing like this happens, everybody skips their meals and their rest; they get so knocked up physically that they can't cope with the situation."

"You're right…I suppose this must be Tucon."

They had entered a broad village street lined with maples; on either side of it trim cottages with gardens had hung out ornamental signs, which Gamadge slowed down to read: "'The Sunflower Studio'; 'Books, Beads, and Baskets'; 'The Jolly Little Shop.' All among the arts and crafts, aren't we? Here we are—'The Pottery Pig.'"

"And there's the turning to the Cove," said Mitchell, as the car stopped. "Right opposite. They've hung up a sign."

The three got out and crossed the road. A large poster, with a lantern hanging above it, swung from a tree. The Gothic lettering ran as follows:

THE OLD PIER PLAYERS

in

YEATS—SYNGE—DUNSANY

To-night at 8.45

"Getting warmer," said Gamadge.

"Will people actually come all the way up here to see this show?" Sanderson was incredulous.

"No doubt; but I'm not absolutely certain that this Callaghan has his finger on the pulse of his public."

He led the way back to the 'Pottery Pig,' which was nothing more than a large barn, set well back from the street, and approached over a rough expanse of half-cut grass. The barn had been allowed to retain its faded red paint, but its big doors were now closed and padlocked. A faintly beaten track led the visitors around the corner to the south side, where a narrow entrance gaped darkly between show windows. The first contained marines, and landscapes in water-colour and oil; the second, pottery.

"My gracious," said Mitchell, staring. "Is that the Pig?"

He might well ask, since its tail alone identified it. It was a monstrous animal, pinkish, highly glazed, and covered with dark spots; it had a kind of scalloped frieze along its back, and its open jaws showed two complete rows of formidable teeth. It was surrounded by a collection of thick, greyish jugs, bowls and basins, fungoid in colour and texture. Very small china animals, pigs for the most part, were scattered among the pottery.

"That must be the Pig." Gamadge tore himself away from contemplation of the really horrid object, and went into the barn, the others following. It was dim and empty, except for a counter to the right, sketches tacked to the walls, and some small chairs and tables grouped near the tall double doors in the rear, through which loads of hay had once been driven.

"Nobody home," said Mitchell. As he spoke, a bead curtain behind the counter clicked, and a dour-looking young man entered. He wore a painter's smock and rope sandals, and there was a palette on his left thumb. His right grasped a large brush, with blue paint on it. Surveying the visitors with every sign of distaste, he asked: "Well? What is it?"

"Lunch," replied Gamadge, in whom rudeness invariably begot brevity.

"Oh. Carrie!" The dour young man shouted the name at the top of his lungs, and a little woman with thin blond hair, a pince-nez attached to a gold chain, and an overall decorated with animals, came in through a door lower down.

"Three lunches, please," said Gamadge.

"Three chicken and waffle dinners," the little woman corrected him briskly.

"That's right."

"We serve coffee and raspberries with them."

"Perfect."

She went out again. The dour young man had turned and was about to butt his way through the bead portière when Mitchell addressed him:

"Say, young feller. You take messages here for Seal Cove?"

The artist swung around, rage in his eye. "You can go down there yourself, and deliver your message," he said furiously.

"Oh, I'm going. I didn't ask you to take one," explained Mitchell. "I asked you if you did take 'em."

"If we'd known it was going to be a whole week, instead of a day or so, we shouldn't have agreed to do it at all. Perfect nuisance," scolded the young man. "I was glad to oblige Callaghan; we have friends in the outfit, and we're doing some of his scenic designing for him. But really, what with the telephone calls and the telegrams, we haven't had a minute's peace. We take the receiver off the hook, now, at night. If we didn't——"

Another youth, short, and with a bumpy forehead and thick tow-coloured hair, appeared in the doorway. He was dressed like his colleague; in fact, exactly like him; but, instead of a palette and brush, he carried a roll of gilt paper and a pair of scissors.

"What's the trouble?" he enquired.

"No trouble, I hope." Mitchell was ominously mild. "I wanted some information. Perhaps you'll furnish it; any reference to telephone messages for the Cove seems to send this friend of yours right off his head."

"You wouldn't be surprised at that, if you knew what it's been like. Now the audience is beginning to call up, asking us what the plays are, and all sorts of things. We don't know what they are," squeaked the tow-headed artist, indignantly. "Callaghan won't say."

"Rather hard on a scenic designer, I should think," murmured Gamadge.

"You don't know that Irishman. 'Atmosphere!' he yells. 'Don't you worry yourselves about atmosphere. There's more atmosphere down on that pier than we can make use of. You just paint me a flight of stairs in perspective, and we'll put the atmosphere in.'"

"Trying."

"All I want to know," persisted Mitchell, "is about that telephone message from the Harbour Inn at Portsmouth, last evening. What time would you say it must have come, Mr. Sanderson?"

"Let's see; about eight, I should think. He was alone, then, for a few minutes. I thought he was asleep. How he ever got the strength, I don't know."

"A telephone call from Portsmouth, about eight o'clock. For Mr. Arthur Atwood."

The taller artist exclaimed, violently: "Do you suppose we remember the things? We've had hundreds——"

"Thousands," said the short one.

"Stuff and nonsense. You had to write messages down, if you meant to deliver 'em. Is Callaghan paying you for the job?"

"Naturally, we are being compensated. The recipients pay him, and he pays us." The dour young man glared at Mitchell. "Of course we deliver the messages."

"How?"

"Send down. They can't expect to get the things in five minutes; but they do, sometimes."

"Well, anyway, you must keep a record. If you'd rather not go into your files now, you can come down to the Centre to-morrow, and give evidence at the inquest. I thought I'd save you the trouble."

"What inquest? What are you talking about?"

"Now, Bobbie!" His tow-headed friend seized him by the arm. "Let me handle this. Who's dead, Mr.—er——"

"Mitchell. The young fellow that put in the telephone call died suddenly, and we want to check up on the message."

"Oh, I see; or rather, I don't. Anyhow, we were both out for supper last night, and there was a dance afterwards at the Sunflower Studio. Bob's still feeling the effects, as you may have noticed. Carrie Gootch stayed on to answer the telephone. Here, Carrie!"

Miss or Mrs. Gootch trotted out of the kitchen, tray in hand. She placed it on one of the tables, and began to distribute cups and plates. Sanderson watched her hungrily.

"Carrie, these people want to know about a telephone call that came in about eight o'clock last night from—where did you say, Mr. Mitchell?"

"Harbour Inn, Portsmouth."

Carrie advanced down the length of the barn. "I sent it along down," she said, peering through her glasses.

Mitchell gave a deep sigh. "So that's that. Now, ma'am, I'd be obliged if you'd give me an idea what he said."

"What did he say?" she meditated, while tension gripped the 'Pottery Pig.'

"You write 'em down, don't you?" Mitchell restrained himself with difficulty from leading the witness. "Think. Young feller in a hotel, trying to get a message—important message—to Mr. Arthur Atwood."

"It wasn't so very important. Let's see. I and the help had washed up, and she had went home; we both live down the street. I fooled around, dusted the china animals and the pig, and sat down to read and wait for ten o'clock."

"You were leaving the place at ten?"

"We take the receiver off the hook then, and don't it make the Oakport operator mad! Well, about eight, the bell rung."

Everybody, including the two painters, held their breath.

"Young feller says: 'This where they take calls for Seal Cove?' I sez: 'Yes, it is.' He says: 'It has to git there to-night.' I sez: 'It will if I can find a boy.' He sez: 'I'll hold the line till you find one.' So I went out back and hollered to Mis' Brown at the 'Jolly Little Shop.' Her boy come running. He does all the odd jobs for us round here, and he takes stuff down to the Cove. I sez to the feller on the phone: 'Here's the boy; now what?' He says: 'Write it down. It's for Arthur Atwood, from Amberley Cowden.' And he spelled it all out for me."

"Too good to be true," said Gamadge to the roof beams. "Things don't happen like this. There's a catch in it, somewhere. It wasn't in code, or anything, was it, Miss—er—Mrs.——"

"Mrs. Carrie Gootch. There wasn't no code, and there wasn't no catch."

Mitchell was jubilant. "Go right ahead and tell us what it said, ma'am. This young feller here has codes on the brain."

"'Mis' Gootch,' he sez. 'Tell him Amberley Cowden's been sick, and we're layin' up for a couple of hours at the Harbour Inn, Portsmouth. Tell him we're goin' to start not later than ten, and we'll git to Ford's Beach to-night. Tell him, plans unchanged.'"

There was a long and painful silence, made still more painful by Gamadge's attempt to hum. At last Mitchell enquired anxiously: "You sure that was all?"

"Every last word."

"But you couldn't be expected to remember it all. If you thought it over ——"

"I don't have to think it over. He spelled out most every other word, like as if I was deaf, or something; and I had to repeat it back to him twice."

"Not a thing about what those plans were, that he wasn't going to change?"

"Not a thing."

"All right. Thanks."

"Your dinner's ready. You ain't goin' to let them waffles cool off, be you?"

"No. Think you can get hold of that Brown boy for us?"

"I kin try." She left by the side door, and the party sat down at their table. Conversation lapsed while they consumed food and coffee, Gamadge merely observing gloomily: "There certainly was a catch, and there may have been a code, after all."

"I don't believe there was a code." Sanderson gulped coffee, and went on: "I think he was just checking up on his plan, as I told you this morning. He'd want to keep Atwood posted right up to date—about his being sick, and being late, and all the rest of it. For all I know, that second call at the Ocean House may not have been camouflage at all; it may just have been another attempt to O.K. the arrangements as made. Of course he'd pretend he didn't know how to get through by way of Tucon." Sanderson drank some more coffee, and added: "He liked to feel that he was behaving in a sophisticated way, you know. I think he would have thought a code silly."

"And that's for you, Mr. Gamadge," Mitchell sputtered.

"Yes. Thanks. Well, your tip worked out, Sanderson; even if it doesn't help much. We know Atwood got a message, and that's the important thing. What's more," said Gamadge, "that fact shifts the whole business to the Cove, and to Atwood."

"Gives us something to tackle him about," agreed Mitchell.

A boy of fourteen jounced across the hand-mown stubble on his bicycle, stopped in front of the doorway, and supported himself with one foot on the sill.

"I couldn't help it, I couldn't help it," he shouted. "Mr. Callaghan took it away from me. Mom says you can't do anything to me."

"What's the trouble, son?" enquired Mitchell.

"Mrs. Gootch says the telephone company is after me for not delivering that telephone message personal."

"You didn't give it to Atwood himself?"

"No, but he got it. I went out on the pier, and Callaghan stopped me at the door. He said Mr. Atwood was busy, and I couldn't go inside. So I just gave him the paper."

"And then what?"

"He went in, and I waited to see if there was an answer. I always do. I heard him say 'Here's a message,' or something like that, and Mr. Atwood said: 'Now what?' And then he said: 'The boy's been sick. He means to come on to-morrow, but I wonder if he'll make it.' Something like that…"

"It was Atwood talking, was it?"

"Yes, it was. I called out, 'Any answer?' And he called back, 'No, I won't bother. All right, kid. Thanks.' Only of course I can't just remember the exact words."

"You're doing fine. Didn't you try to see indoors?"

"No. I've seen inside that theatre lots of times. Nothing to see. It's only an old fish-house."

"And then you left, did you?"

"Mr. Callaghan came out and paid me, and asked me if the fog was bad in the lane yet. I said it was, but my lamp's a good new one, and I could see good enough. I started down the gangway, and Mr. Callaghan stood in the door. He called back inside: 'Don't you think you ought to try and get in touch with him?' And I heard Mr. Atwood call back: 'No, let it stay right there on the knees of the gods.' I've taken lots of messages down to him; I'd know his voice any place."

"Is he given to classical allusion?" asked Gamadge, amused.

"Yes, he's always funny."

Mrs. Gootch came up, disapproval gleaming through her pince-nez. "I say you hadn't ought to have delivered that paper to anybody but the feller himself, Lefty Brown," she declared. "Suppose it had been a private message, and this manager had read it? That ain't right. The telephone company——"

"Let's forget the telephone company, Miss Gootch," said Mitchell. "They haven't any more to do with this than that pig in the window. The responsibility, if there is any, rests with you people here. If you want personal delivery insured, you send a man down. This boy did the best he could."

Lefty, who seemed more relieved than triumphant, turned his bicycle and careened off toward the 'Jolly Little Shop.' Mrs. Gootch cleared away the plates, removed them to the kitchen, and returned with saucers of raspberries and wedges of chocolate cake.

"She may be confused in her ideas," said Mitchell, after an interval, "but there isn't a thing the matter with her cooking."

"I feel like another person." Sanderson finished his third cup of coffee, and leaned backwards against the barn wall. "You're right; I was starving."

"Too bad not to sit here and digest that dinner. I certainly enjoyed it, Mr. Gamadge," said Mitchell. "But we got to be going."

Gamadge found Mrs. Gootch, paid and tipped her, and assured her that he would come again. Then he followed the others to the car.

"Easy, now," begged Mitchell, as they turned into the lane. "This road's a terror, always was. Watch the bends."

The sandy track, hedged in by crowding pines and birches, wound steeply downhill. It was unfurnished with lamps, and in every turn it seemed to be provided with a shoulder of bare rock.

"Is this really the only way out to the Cove?" asked Sanderson.

"Yes, it is," replied Mitchell.

"The whole thing strikes me more and more as a singularly desperate theatrical enterprise," said Gamadge.

"They say summer folks like to explore." Mitchell sniffed the pine and salt laden air. "Smells nice, anyhow."

Bayberry and wild rose mingled with sea-beach odours as the car emerged from the lane and came out in a large clearing. This was bounded on three sides by forest, on the fourth by dazzling blue water; at the edge of the trees on the right was a group of trailers—neat houses on wheels, their steps facing the woods. Opposite them, across the clearing, were tents, and a long row of cars. A narrow gangway led from the shore out to a big, barnlike structure, whence proceeded sounds of immense activity; hammering, shouting, and the metallic bray of barbaric music. The old pier was completely surrounded by water, which came up to within a foot or two of its floor beams; the tops of the piles on which it had been built looked as fragile as cobwebs.

“So that’s the theatre.” Sanderson, having climbed out of the coupé, stood staring at the weatherworn façade, with its gaping doorway.

“That’s it. I suppose, with all this water around, they don’t feel the need of any fire laws up here.” Mitchell walked to the left, and thoughtfully surveyed the row of glassless, shuttered windows. “You jump in the water, or you climb down the piles to the sand depending on the state of the tide. No gallery, nor anything; just that door. Well, well.”

He turned, and glanced curiously about him. The only human beings in sight were some men in jeans, working at a telephone pole behind the last trailer, down by the shore; and a solitary female figure in the middle of the clearing, sitting motionless on a stump.

CHAPTER SEVEN
Mr. Atwood Performs

As they approached, she watched them steadily; but she showed no other sign of interest until, evidently recognising Sanderson, she called out in a deep contralto voice with a rasp in it: "Where's the boy?"

"I'm sorry to bring you bad news, Mrs. Atwood." Sanderson was abrupt, though civil enough. "He's dead."

Mrs. Atwood's expression, which seemed normally to be one of faint disgust, did not alter. She was a woman in her late thirties, thin, large-boned, with a long, narrow face. Her features were badly modelled, her teeth lightly prominent, and her hair a dull and improbable yellow; but somehow she contrived to look handsome. She had made no concession whatever to the picnic conditions about her; being dressed in a figured silk costume, pale silk stockings, high-heeled slippers without toes, and an extraordinary hat like a fragment of rolled-up towelling. She was brilliantly made up, and long green earrings hung from her ears.

After a moment she remarked: "Well; it was bound to happen."

"If you hadn't encouraged him in this theatre idea, perhaps it might not have happened quite so soon, or in quite such a ghastly way." Sanderson's tone was bitter.

"You think I encouraged him?" She allowed her gaze to wander from him to Mitchell and Gamadge. "I don't know what you're talking about. Instead of throwing blame around, you might explain."

"And you might introduce us," suggested Mitchell. Sanderson did so, without amenities. A pretty little girl in a gingham play suit and sandals ran up, and called: "Hello, Mr. Sanderson. Where's Amby?"

Sanderson got out his handkerchief, and mopped his forehead with it. "I'm sorry, Miss Baker…"

"Oh, dear, couldn't he come after all?"

"No, he couldn't."

"Arthur Atwood said he'd been sick again. Is it serious?"

"I'm awfully sorry; he died last night."

Miss Baker gave a childlike wail, and then burst out crying. Mrs. Atwood put out a large, ringed hand, and patted her shoulder. "Now, kid," she said, "you knew it was bound to come. You go get hold of Arthur, and tell Callaghan."

The girl ran off to the gangway, swerving, as she reached it, to avoid a slight figure that had just emerged from the entrance to the pier. Mrs. Atwood raised her voice to a volume of sound capable, Gamadge thought, of overflowing Madison Square Garden.

"Come up here, Art," she called, "and see how your racket turned out."

Mr. Atwood, who was clothed lightly in a pair of bathing shorts and a bath towel, advanced in a series of bounds and leaps across the short, dry grass. He sprang into the air with almost inhuman agility, and came down like a feather; arriving finally in a swift rush, and ending it on one knee. He then rose, removed sand from the knee with a corner of the towel, draped it about his shoulders with one wide and wing-like gesture, and said, glancing bird-like from one face to the other:

"Mr. Sanderson and two strangers. Something tells me that the news is going to be bad. Is that what you meant, darling?"

"Don't be an ass," said his wife roughly. "The boy's dead."

"Oh dear me," said Mr. Atwood. In spite of his prowess as a dancer, he did not look young; there were wrinkles at the corners of his dark, half-closed eyes, and the hair above his narrow, sloping forehead was thin. He smiled widely at Sanderson, took a pair of sunglasses from a pocket in his shorts, put them on, and blinked behind them. "That's a blow," he went on in his reedy voice.

"It certainly is," said his wife, drily. "I knew I was a fool when I turned down that tour with the musical show; but Callaghan isn't as well prepared as I was. He won't like it."

"My dear child!" Atwood addressed her in a tone of mild rebuke. "It's all very well to be a realist; I hope I am one myself; but, after all, the blow is not, to me, financial. When did it happen?" He spoke to Sanderson, but his eyes, behind the dark glasses, were on Gamadge. They moved from him to Mitchell, and back again.

Mitchell answered: "Probably about two this morning."

"Well, I'm thankful it didn't happen up here," remarked Mrs. Atwood. "I always said the whole idea was crazy. His family would have sued us for manslaughter."

"My idea," explained Atwood, who seemed to be strung on wires, so continual and puppet-like were the movements of his hands, arms, legs and feet, "my considered opinion was that it didn't really matter where it happened, just so that the unfortunate kid got a little fun. He agreed with me, but hardly anyone else did."

"Well, I'm glad he died in his bed," declared Mrs. Atwood, harshly.

"He didn't die in his bed, Mrs. Atwood," said Mitchell.

"Didn't?" Atwood gazed up at him, the changing mask of his face all interest. "How did it happen, then?"

"The boy fell off a cliff."

"Fell off a cliff!" The lithe figure became rigid, and the eyes behind the sunglasses widened to a stare. "What in the world was he doing on a cliff at two in the morning?"

"We hoped you could tell us that."

"Me?" Atwood stepped back a pace, and looked from one to the other of them, finishing with a bland gaze at his wife, who ignored it stonily.

"Yes. It has been suggested that he was waiting down there for you to pick him up."

"My dear man, you've got it all wrong. There was no arrangement of that sort; naturally not. He was to come up to-day. My goodness me!" Atwood's voice, expressing hurt amazement, turned to a bleat. "Who was kind enough to suggest that idea? You, perhaps?" and he whirled on Sanderson. "Or my cousin Fred? You two knew all about our plans."

"Nobody can imagine why he went down there to that rock," answered Sanderson, coldly. "We thought he might have made some other arrangement with you. When he telephoned, you know. Yesterday."

"Oh. Do you know," said Atwood, his head on one side and an indescribably coy expression on his face, "I thought that telephone call was a private one."

"Nothing stays private in an investigation like this," Mitchell informed him.

"It's an investigation, is it? Oh, I see; he was killed by the fall. Now that is what I call one of life's major ironies; don't you agree with me, Floss?"

"He was probably dead before he went over the cliff, Mr. Atwood; but there will be an inquest, and, of course, we want information."

"Of course you do; so do I. The thing is so dashed queer that I feel completely dazed by it. Where was this cliff?"

"Just below the hotel."

"I don't know Ford's Beach; don't know it at all. He telephoned me—as you probably know already—that the party was getting in late; I suppose as late as midnight?"

"Later."

"And he is imagined to have celebrated his coming of age by going out and falling off a cliff. Poor old Amby. Well, I wish I could help you to clarify the situation; but I cannot. I was rehearsing until after ten o'clock, and then I was sunk in a dreamless sleep. We've had a little sickness in camp," he went on, his thin mouth stretching in a smile, "and it's put extra work on us all. The troupe isn't big; we don't merely double, here; we triple and quadruple."

"Which tent is yours?"

"That one, down beside the water. Desirable situation; lovely fragrance of dead crab when the tide's out. I'm alone in it; my cousin Amberley was going to share it with me," he ended, in a tone of melancholy.

"You were going to put that sick feller to sleep in a tent?"

"He was looking forward to it. Twice as comfortable as a trailer. I hoped the family would let him have a day or two of it, before they drove up with a writ of *habeas corpus*."

"He was of age," Sanderson reminded him, shortly.

"So he was, so he was. He wasn't banking too heavily on that fact, though; he thought they'd declare him irresponsible, or something, before they let go of him. That reminds me," and Atwood turned his wide grin on Sanderson. "Did he get around to signing that will, and getting it witnessed? No such luck, I'm afraid?"

"I didn't know you knew about the will."

"Oh, bless you, he talked of nothing else."

"He probably never did get it signed or witnessed; but whether or not he did, it's gone."

"Gone? Gone where?"

"Disappeared."

Atwood gazed at him, took off his glasses to look down at his wife, put them on again, and shook his head. "There goes our old age pension, Flo," he murmured, "right down the drain. We might have known they'd never let him—ahem. Must be careful not to give voice to unfounded allegations."

Sanderson, looking very angry, began: "What do you mean?" But Gamadge, speaking for the first time, interrupted him. He had been standing in an easy and relaxed posture, watching Atwood with a good deal of interest and some amusement; and he now said, casually:

"Miss Cowden wishes you to be informed that she is carrying out the bequests."

Atwood's dark glasses flashed as he turned them on Gamadge. "What's that you say?"

"Miss Cowden will pay the beneficiaries when she has control of the money."

Atwood immediately seized the towel by both ends, waved it over his head as if it were a scarf, and sprang into the air. He executed an entrechat, and came down on his toes with a delicate precision that somehow made him seem lighter than flesh and blood. This manœuvre was accompanied by a wild yodel in falsetto, the suddenness of which made everybody start. As he stood poised, muscles bunched under a skin which the sun evidently had no power to burn, the sea grass betrayed him; he slipped, clutched at nothing, and landed on all fours.

It may have been a tribute to something or other about Atwood that nobody laughed. He himself seemed rather amused than disconcerted, rose nimbly, and bowed before Gamadge, his towel sweeping the ground.

"Whoever you are, dear old bean," he said, "you bring fair tidings. Wait, though; I see a cloud on the horizon, and it's a damn' sight bigger than a man's hand. Alma's only nineteen. She won't get hold of her capital for two years. Nobody ever gave money away after thinking it over for two years."

"If Miss Cowden says she'll do it, she will do it," Sanderson broke in, sharply.

"Well, you probably know her better than I do, even if I am her nearest living relative, except for Fred. And my aunt Lulu, of course. How does Cousin Fred feel about all this, by the way? Badly cut up, or taking it calmly, as usual? You know," said Atwood, as if reflectively, "I walloped that big brute, once."

"Queensberry rules?" enquired Sanderson.

"I was very young at the time, and Queensberry rules were not in my bright lexicon. Ah, well; one hundred thousand dollars, what's that? Illusion. But if you listen closely, you will hear the gnashing of my wife's teeth."

Gamadge asked: "Is the word *hubris* in your bright lexicon?"

Atwood paused, turned his head, and looked sharply at the speaker. "What's that?" he demanded.

"*Hubris*."

"Oh, I know what it means; I went to night school. So you think I'm a bit above myself, do you?"

"A trifle, perhaps."

"You may be right; it's reaction. I've had several shocks, you know; or, rather, you don't. Excuse me, but did I hear anybody mention who you happen to be?"

"Slight acquaintance of your family," replied Gamadge.

"To whom my cousin Alma confides her financial intentions, and whom she sends forth as minister plenipotentiary, to convey them to her relatives. And what, Mr. Hugh Sanderson, do you think of that? Don't bother to tell me, though, because here is Callaghan, whom I could find it in my heart to pity."

Callaghan, followed by a dozen young men and women, came slowly towards them from the shore. He was a big, redheaded Irishman, in corduroys and a grimy white sweater; and his troupe were all clad in the extreme of beach undress. Slacks, bathing suits and shorts predominated; none of the youths wore anything above the waist, and the girls very little. They stopped at a short distance, and the manager came on alone. Miss Baker brought up the rear with a stalwart in red canvas trousers, whose great arm, tanned like leather, was about her shoulders.

"What's this I hear?" demanded Callaghan.

Atwood performed introductions:

"Allow me to present our director, Mr. James Callaghan, who is steeped in the traditions of the Abbey Theatre, Dublin. He has but one fault, if it be a fault: he has an almost pathological addiction to the Irish drama. Callaghan, this is Mr. Sanderson, my cousin Amberley's tutor and friend. His best friend, I believe; common justice impels me to say so. These other gentlemen have not obliged me with their names; but I should judge that the older one is connected in some way with the law. The other says he is slightly acquainted with the Cowden family, and his part in these events remains obscure."

"I'm Mitchell, state detective," said Mitchell. "This is Mr. Gamadge."

"Oh," said Callaghan. He looked at Mitchell oddly. "You're up here about the death of this boy?"

"Yes."

"Well, the Lord be thanked he didn't die here; we might have had all kinds of trouble over it. It's bad enough the way it is, with me shorthanded already, and most of these boys and girls amateurs that wouldn't know how to cover up a state wait, much less take a part at short notice. What are we to do now, Atwood? You got me into this. You never told me this Cowden boy was in immediate danger of dying."

"I didn't know it myself; he's been the same, on and off, for years. Delighted to carry his spear for him, in addition to my other chores," replied Atwood cheerfully. "I'm only in two of the plays now; put me in the third, by all means. It's all one to me."

Mrs. Atwood broke her long silence with some asperity: "If you'd let me have Adrienne's part, you wouldn't be in any trouble at all. Susie Baker, or any of the girls, could do mine."

"We've had that all out a dozen times, Floss." Callaghan patted her on the shoulder with amiable detachment. "It's all settled. Sure, you'd blast the audience out of their seats in the Yeats play."

"It's a heavy part; when it's played properly."

"You have the heaviest part in the whole show; be satisfied with it, and leave me in peace."

Atwood, who had for some reason been smirking complacently, now asked: "Don't you want to know why a state detective came all the way up here to break the news to us?"

"I'm not sure that I do."

"It's really very interesting, though; my cousin Amberley appears to have left the hotel at two o'clock in the morning, gone down and climbed on some cliff or other, had a fatal attack, and fallen on to the rocks. What do you make of that?"

"What do you want me to make of it?"

"I wish you would make something; because my family, the dear creatures, are trying at last to get me into the domestic picture. They seemed to have suggested that I drove down there to meet the boy."

Callaghan looked surprised. "He was to come up to-day."

"We all know that; the idea is that there was a last-minute change of plan. Now you saw that message I got last night; and you know it was the only message I did get. Was there any change of plan mentioned in it?"

"So far as I can remember it, the boy said nothing about a change of plan. He said the plan was to remain unchanged."

"Whereupon I went on rehearsing, out there on the pier, until I staggered to my tent at ten o'clock, or thereabouts?"

"You were busy enough up to ten," agreed Callaghan, "and then you were in your tent, which is next to mine, for my sins, and plenty of noise you make in it. But whether you stayed in it for the rest of the night, the Devil himself only knows."

"Very helpful, you are," complained Atwood, looking grieved. "How about this? We all know the kind of racket that old pram of mine makes, getting out of this dump; did you, or any of you," and he addressed the group of actors beyond Callaghan, "hear me leave the place at any time last night?... No? I thought not. Give it up, Mr. Mitchell; there's nothing in the notion, nothing at all."

Gamadge said: "Why the intensive rehearsing, Mr. Atwood?"

"Ah, that's telling! Come up to the show and find out—if you can."

"I shall certainly try to do that."

"We're just trying to account for the boy going down to that cliff," explained Mitchell. "His death is a financial disappointment for you, I understand, Mr. Callaghan?"

"You can call it that. He was supposed to be bringing money into the enterprise, but I knew he was not well, and I looked upon it as a gamble. Atwood, here, always has some scheme or other on hand. Some of them come off, some of them do not. The boy's death is just another bad luck turn; and if I was a superstitious man, it might upset me."

"Why so?" asked Gamadge.

Callaghan, without replying, nodded as if to call his attention to something beyond. He turned, as did the others, in time to see the entrance from the lane of a most extraordinary cavalcade. It was headed by a policeman on a motorcycle; behind him came a sedan, with two men in it; and last of all lumbered a rusty black vehicle, looking wildly incongruous in that scene of sunlight, pines, blue sky and blue water.

"Good Lord Almighty!" said Mitchell. "It's a hearse."

CHAPTER EIGHT
Sleep for an Actress

The procession came to a stop, and a short, stout man alighted from the sedan. He waddled across the intervening space, while his companion, aided by the driver of the hearse, began to unload cases from the back of the car.

"Stole a march on us, did you, Mitchell?" The stout man came up, and glanced about him at the assembled company. "Where's the manager of this aggregation, and where's the body?"

Mitchell did not reply; Gamadge, after a look at him, decided that he actually couldn't, his rage and astonishment were too great. Callaghan said:

"Over there in the last trailer."

"You didn't think it was worth mentioning?" Mitchell regarded him with cold fury.

"I haven't had a chance to mention it. I sent one of the boys up to Tucon with a message for the sheriff as soon as we found her."

"Her? Who?" barked Mitchell.

"Adrienne Lake—one of our actresses."

"When did she die, and what of?"

"I don't know when, and I don't know why; unless she took too much sleeping stuff. She's had a bad tooth."

"And when did you find out that she was dead?"

"Not until an hour ago. None of us saw her after seven o'clock, last night. She turned in then. Said she couldn't play to-night unless the abscess had gone down. Nobody bothered her this morning." He turned to the stout man, who had been listening to this with a judicial expression. "You're the medical examiner?"

"That's who I am. Cogswell."

"We open to-night, you know; at least, we mean to—if the skies don't fall on us. Can you keep this thing quiet till to-morrow?"

"You fight that out with Mitchell and the sheriff. Come on, boys, we'd better get going."

He went down to the trailer Callaghan had indicated; it stood at the end of the line, near the edge of the steep bank that descended to the pebbly beach. His assistants followed him, casting curious glances at the group of silent actors. Mitchell continued to gaze at Callaghan, who went on gloomily:

"We have three experienced actresses here—had, I mean—and Adrienne, poor girl, was the best of the lot. A nice hole her death has put me in. It's not much to ask; just to keep it out of the news till tomorrow."

"You show folks have me beat. What's this stuff you say she's been taking?"

"I couldn't tell you the name of it. Something the dentist gave her, in case her teeth kept her awake at night. She's had no proper sleep for a week, poor thing, but it wasn't until yesterday that she gave up her part."

"How was it nobody looked in to see how she was getting along?"

"Sure, none of us would have had the heart to disturb her. We live pretty much as we like, up here; we pick up meals in the cook tent when we want them. For all I knew, she'd had her breakfast. Susie Baker, here, slept in the trailer with her, and noticed nothing out of the way."

Mitchell followed his gesture, and addressed the little blond girl, who came forward accompanied by her muscular friend.

"You and Callaghan come down to that trailer with me. I want to get this straight."

The young man beside her stepped forward; he had a dish towel in one hand; the other was clasped loosely about Miss Baker's upper arm.

"I'll stick around with Susie," he said.

"Who're you?"

"My name's Rogers. George Rogers."

"You the cook?"

"We all cook. I was washing the dinner dishes."

"You go on back and wash 'em. Now, Miss Baker."

"I'll just stick around."

"You'll do as I say."

"Please let George come with me," said Miss Baker, tears rolling down her cheeks.

"She's had a terrible shock, finding Miss Lake dead; and then hearing about this Cowden feller on top of it. I come from her home town," said Mr. Rogers. "I'm sort of looking out for her."

"Well, come on, then. Over here." Mitchell led the way to the nearest trailer. "Sit down on the steps, Miss Baker," he said, irritably. She obeyed him, and the interrogation proceeded in full committee. "You tell me you slept all night in that caravan with that dead woman, and never knew the difference?"

"She was behind the curtain," wept Miss Baker.

"You didn't ask her how she was, or offer to get her anything?"

"I knew she'd taken the medicine. I wouldn't have bothered her for anything."

"How about this morning?"

"I got up early, and came out without making any noise."

"So, as far as you or anybody knows, she may have been dead since a little after seven last night?"

Miss Baker nodded, and buried her face in her arms.

"Well, never mind. Stay around, now, and I'll talk to you again, later."

Atwood had been standing on one leg, looking very birdlike indeed with his cocked head, long neck and beaky nose. He now said, gazing affectionately at Miss Baker:

"This young lady, Mr. Mitchell, is well-known to my wife and myself; in fact, we got her the job with Callaghan. She met Amberley Cowden at our place in

New York, and so did Mr. Rogers. We know all about Susie. If she says she doesn't know anything about the death of our leading lady, you may take her word for it."

"Thanks," said Mitchell. He looked at the troupe of actors, and said shortly: "You people are not to go off this place till further notice, understand? Not one of you. I'm leaving that state policeman up here to take care of you."

"If any of us made an effort to leave the place before to-night's performance," Atwood informed him, "Callaghan would kill us. Wouldn't you, old boy? I don't think you quite realise," he went on, eyeing Mitchell quizzically, "what all these calamities mean to our manager. To us all. Don't blame us for slight tendencies towards hysteria. Do you mind very much if I go and take my dip, now? I really feel the need of it, and tides wait for no man. This one will slide out on me, if I don't grab it pretty soon."

"Go ahead."

Atwood skipped away, and Mitchell, with Callaghan beside him, moved off in the direction of the mortuary trailer. Sanderson addressed Miss Baker sympathetically:

"Hard on you, Susie. And I know you feel badly about Amberley. But he couldn't have lived long, in any case—you knew that."

"It's so awful, his falling off that cliff."

"He died before he fell, or so they say."

"Yes, but why did he ever go and climb up on a cliff, in the middle of the night?" She looked up, and caught Gamadge's eye. "Did you know him?" she asked.

"Slightly."

"Don't you think it was funny for him to do a thing like that?"

"It was the last thing I should have expected him to do."

"He was so careful of himself. But he was awfully nice. George liked him, didn't you, George?"

"Yes, I did; the poor kid."

"He did want to come up here with us this summer. I suppose he really couldn't have stood it."

"You can stand a good deal, if you're happy," said Gamadge.

Miss Baker watched Mrs. Atwood get up from her stump and wander down towards the gangway. The others also had dispersed; the state policeman stood for a few moments alone and undecided, and then wheeled his motorcycle under a tree, and sat down.

"Mrs. Atwood is nice," said Miss Baker. "She's ever so much nicer than she looks."

Sanderson smiled, but Gamadge replied, seriously: "She is nice; I agree with you."

"Amby was fond of her. Oh, it's too bad he couldn't live to do all the things he was going to do, Mr. Gamadge! He was going to buy us real scenery, and help Mr. Callaghan to put on good plays. If the season had turned out well, he was going to pay us younger ones salaries."

"You don't get salaries now, Miss Baker?"

"Oh, no; just our board and keep, while we're learning. We get the experience, you see."

"I see. Then you all go back to New York in the fall, and get Broadway engagements."

"Yes," replied Miss Baker, simply. "I will, anyway. George and some of the others are only doing it for fun, in their vacations. He didn't plan to come at all, but Mother thought it would be nice for me to have somebody here that I knew."

"And Mr. Rogers agreed with her."

Young Rogers muttered something. Susie, after a glance at him, explained:

"He wants me to—he thinks I ought to—oh, dear! It does seem so mean."

"What does?"

"Telling on anybody, and Mrs. Atwood has been so nice to me."

Rogers said: "You go ahead and tell that detective."

"I hate to do it. All you think about is my interests, but I have to consider other things. I'll ask Mr. Sanderson what he thinks."

"If you do, he'll simply go and tell the man himself."

"You won't, Mr. Sanderson, will you? Not if I ask you not to?"

"Not unless you bumped this poor Miss Lake off yourself, or anything like that," Sanderson assured her.

"It has nothing to do with me; or not much of anything. You see, last night there was a dance up at Tucon, in one of the studios. I know some of the people up there, and they asked me to go. Two boys that paint and draw. They've done some of our scenery."

"We've met them," Sanderson told her, grimly. "At least we have if they own the 'Spotted Pig.'"

"'The Pottery Pig,' you mean. They don't own it, Mr. Sanderson; Mrs. Gootch owns it. They just rent some of it from her."

"Bums," said Rogers.

"No, they're very nice boys, only last night they both took too much to drink, and there wasn't anybody to bring me home."

"Where was Rogers?" Sanderson looked at him reproachfully.

"He wasn't asked, because he's always telling me it's time to go home, or something. I didn't tell him a word about the party; I just went up by myself, on foot."

"That's a nice way to treat your chaperon, I must say."

"You can laugh," growled Rogers. "See what she got herself into, before you decide it's so funny."

Gamadge said: "Now, now. Of course it's funny—so far. What happened, Miss Baker? You had to tackle that lane alone, late on a foggy night. Deplorable experience; it must have been a brute of a walk."

"It was. I was never so scared in my life. If I'd known that she was dead, in that trailer!..."

"Perhaps she wasn't, then."

"But I realise now that she didn't make a sound. It was too quiet! Well, they're small, you know, those trailers are; you can't help bumping around inside them; so I thought I'd undress outside, so I shouldn't disturb her. I took my clothes off, behind the trees just next to the step; and then, just as I was going in, I heard a car."

She stopped, looking so frightened that Rogers placed a huge hand on her arm, and bade her take it easy.

"I wasn't scared then; I thought somebody else had sneaked off, just as I had. You see, Mr. Callaghan won't let us go off the place and stay up late, without permission. He's always afraid something will happen to interfere with the opening. He said he'd fire anybody that wasn't at the Cove by ten o'clock. Well, this car came out of the lane, and I peeked round the tree to see who it was. It hardly made any sound, and its lights were off, and the fog was thick; but I recognised his old Ford."

"Whose old Ford?" asked Gamadge.

"Mr. Atwood's. He drove across and left it on the lane, and he never even shut the door, for fear he'd make a noise. He just left it hanging open, and slid over to his tent."

"What time was this, Miss Baker?"

"Nearly three o'clock."

Gamadge and Sanderson exchanged a look. The latter asked: "You're sure it was Atwood?"

"Well, he went into Mr. Atwood's tent, and it was his car."

There was a pause. Then Sanderson asked: "Mightn't he have been off on the quiet, at some party of his own?"

"The rules don't apply to the Atwoods. They're partners, or something. They come and go as they like. I just wondered whether he did go down there to meet Amby, and—and——"

"Young Cowden seems to have died a natural death, Miss Susie," said Gamadge, gently. "And Atwood doesn't seem to have gained anything by it."

"I know."

"But you don't understand why Atwood should deny being off the place, and you don't like him, and you want to get at the bottom of what happened to your friend. Quite right. Well, you haven't asked my advice, but I'm going to offer it, just the same. Tell Mitchell."

"That's my advice, too," said Sanderson. "And Rogers', I believe."

"She'd be crazy to keep it to herself," said Rogers.

"Yes, but Mr. Atwood will be sure to find out who told. He always finds out everything. He knows the 'Pottery Pig' boys, and he'll hear that I came home alone from that party." Susie Baker was almost trembling; certainly the hand that seized Rogers' sleeve was not steady.

"The fellow certainly has an extraordinary faculty for inspiring terror," said Gamadge. "At first glance, you'd call him a moderately clever little exhibitionist."

"More than that, I think," said Sanderson.

"Well, I haven't really had my second glance yet. If you're afraid of him, Miss Baker, you know what to do; stay with the crowd from now on. Don't wander off by yourself, not for a minute. Hang on to young Rogers here like grim death. Where are you sleeping, now?"

"I'm going to be in with Mrs. Atwood."

"Does that arrangement satisfy you?"

"Oh, yes. Besides, there's another girl in there already. I'm going to sleep on the floor."

"Good. And don't forget that Mitchell's leaving a trooper here for the present."

"If I tell Mr. Mitchell, Mr. Atwood will see me talking to him."

"I'll tell Mitchell myself."

Gamadge strolled down to the last trailer, against the side of which Callaghan leaned, sunk in dismal contemplation.

"Too bad this had to happen to you, Mr. Callaghan," he said.

"You don't know half of it. If her relations don't get my telegrams, or don't come forward, who's to pay the funeral expenses?"

"Had Miss Lake no money?"

"She was always hard up, poor girl. If she had had any money she wouldn't have been here, living in a caravan. It was no life for her, at her age; but she asked me for the job, to tide her over. She was Irish, you know. She'd played in these plays all her life."

"I saw her in one, once. Quite a distinguished actress, at one time, wasn't she?"

"She was, but the poor creature had her troubles. Well, she has a niece in the pictures, and her brother travels in wallpaper; I got their addresses out of her little bag, and the medical examiner goes on as if I'd robbed the corpse."

"You didn't do that." Dr. Cogswell's large head protruded from the little window above their heads. "We found fifty dollars under her pillow."

"Fifty—what are you telling me? Didn't she borrow five dollars yesterday from little Susie Baker?"

"Then she put one over. I'm keeping this money, Callaghan, but you'll get a receipt for it."

"Will it pay for a decent funeral, Doctor? I can add a little to it, but we're not made of money, up here. I don't want her buried on the parish."

"Don't worry; we'll fix her up some way. Would you say she might have got sick of the whole business, and taken an overdose of this stuff on purpose?" He exhibited a small bottle, containing a few tablets and a lump of cotton.

"God forbid! I don't think so. She was interested in our theatre here, and she was an old trouper, and liked her parts. Her toothache was wearing her down, but she meant to go on with her work when the swelling left her."

Mitchell's face appeared beside Cogswell's. "Did you say you saw Miss Lake on the stage?" he asked Gamadge.

"Yes. Long ago."

"Come in and see her now."

As he spoke, Cogswell's two assistants came down the steps and went off in the direction of the hearse. Gamadge entered the little house on wheels, and walked up to the end of it, where one narrow shelf-like bunk hung out from the wall. Cogswell and Mitchell stood beside it, and Cogswell turned the sheet back from a small, darkly coloured, peaceful face.

"She's had morphia," he said, "and plenty of it. See that colour? See those pupils?" He turned back an eyelid. "She's been dead, going on twelve hours."

Gamadge looked down at what remained of Miss Adrienne Lake. She had been, as he remembered her, a coquettish type of actress; but she had cast off ancient coquetries at Seal Cove. She wore a high-necked, long-sleeved flannel nightdress, and her sparse brown hair was tied up in a bandanna handkerchief; she looked old, tired and poor. The left side of her face was slightly swollen.

"You can identify her?" asked Mitchell.

"Certainly. She's a finer-looking woman at this moment, if you can believe it, than she ever was; but perhaps I think so because I never did care for her type of face. Small, wide across the top, pointed chin, big eyes, short nose, full mouth. Rather sly, I thought she looked; but that's gone now. She has dignity."

"You'd be surprised how many of 'em have, when it's all over."

The two assistants arrived with a stretcher, and Gamadge left the trailer. Mitchell followed him. As they joined Callaghan, Cogswell put his head again out of the window.

"That myocarditis case, Mitchell," he said. "Baines is on it."

"Good."

"We'll have a full report for you in a couple of hours, now."

"Thanks."

"Angel of death seems to be operating in this vicinity at a great rate. Did you say one of those actors is a cousin of the Cowden boy?"

"Yes."

"Quite a coincidence."

"Quite."

Callaghan interrupted this colloquy. "We're opening to-night, you know. Don't tell me we can't open to-night."

"Nobody wants to create unnecessary hardships for you."

"If they're turned back to-night, they won't come again. Hardships! It'll be ruin. Why won't you arrange to keep the thing quiet for twelve hours?"

"We can't shove her into the ground and forget about it, Callaghan; this wasn't a natural death. You show people do beat all."

"She'd be the last to want the season ruined, God rest her soul."

"Go ahead with your entertainment; but I'm leaving a man to guard this trailer till we get it printed, and another at the top of the lane. I want your people to stay on these premises for the present. There'll be an inquest, of course."

"One or more," said Callaghan.

"What do you mean?"

"They say these things go by threes. Wasn't I telling you it might make a superstitious man worry? Not that there's any connection between poor old Adrienne

Lake and that dead boy."

"Your show and that dead boy are connected. I want your troupe to stay right here on the spot."

"What for, in the name of nonsense? Oh, well; have it your own way. They're not likely to get off the place, with all they have ahead of them now. We do our own scene-shifting."

Gamadge conducted Mitchell across the clearing to his car. He there unfolded Susie Baker's story, which Mitchell received with a grunt of bafflement.

"I'll talk to the feller," he said, "and much good it will do. He's as slippery as an eel. The girl never even saw him, and when he finds that out, he'll have us where he wants us."

"He has you where he wants you now. He has you all hypnotised."

"Why should he, or anybody else, make away with this poor actress? Callaghan says she hadn't an enemy in the world, much less at the Cove. Who benefits by her death, I'd like to know?"

"Nobody but her understudy, I should think. Are you coming back to the Beach with us?"

"No. Cogswell's driving me to the Centre."

Sanderson approached. "Going?" he asked.

"All ready."

Sanderson got into the car, and Gamadge slid behind the wheel. Mitchell glowered at the glittering waters of the Cove.

"Wonder if Laroche will have to take off his clothes and wade out after Atwood," he reflected, aloud. "There's at least six swimmers out there; pretty far out, too. Hey, Laroche."

The trooper woke from his doze under the tree, and got to his feet; but Atwood's reedy voice said at Mitchell's elbow: "No need to call up the reserves. Here I am, right on the carpet."

The suddenness of his appearance suggested that he had sprung from the ground. Mitchell, turning on him, asked with the irritability of one who has been startled: "Where'd you come from?"

"From behind Mr. Gamadge's car. I've been admiring it, and also doing a teeny-weeny bit of eavesdropping. You wouldn't blame me, would you?"

Mitchell flapped a hand at the state policeman, meanwhile gazing at the innocent face of his questioner with deep annoyance. Mr. Atwood, who was now dressed in a green shirt, pale fawn-coloured trousers, and brown-and-white sport shoes, leaned an arm on the sill of the car window next to Gamadge, and returned the look, blandly.

"A lizard; that's what he reminds me of," reflected Gamadge, and said aloud, "Perhaps it's the green shirt, though."

"You don't care for it?" The narrow eyes, all but closed against the afternoon glare, slid sideways. Gamadge said:

"Excuse me. I didn't realise that I was thinking aloud. Very striking. Just the colour of a chameleon I had once."

"I dress the part. Don't you recognise in me, Mr. Gamadge, a spirit of air and fire?" asked Atwood, plaintively. "Callaghan says I'm a leprechaun."

"He may be right." Gamadge considered him thoughtfully.

"You, Mr. Gamadge, consider yourself wiser than the children of light, do you not?"

"Far from it. Could you be persuaded to shed your Elemental qualities for a minute or two, and help us over a little difficulty we find ourselves in?"

"Delighted, if I can; but I'm afraid I can't."

Mitchell burst out impatiently: "Why can't you come out with it, and admit that you went down there last night to meet the boy? It needn't get you into any trouble."

"Oh, no; of course not." Atwood looked amused.

"Perhaps you never saw him at all. He might have died and gone over the edge of the rock before you showed up. All we want is information—for the inquest," continued Mitchell, persuasively. "Otherwise, those ladies might be kept hanging around here for days. We don't want to adjourn the inquest."

"That would be a shame, I agree."

"Then why not make it easy for us, and everybody concerned, and admit he was on that cliff waiting for you?"

"You wouldn't want me to perjure myself, I hope?"

"If you'd be perjuring yourself by saying that, I'll retire and sacrifice my pension."

"Any particular reason for this certainty, or is it merely wishful thinking?"

"You are known to have been off the place, last night."

"Seen somewhere else, was I?"

"Do you deny that you drove your car back in here shortly before three o'clock?"

Atwood's sharp attention relaxed; he smiled widely, and replied: "No, I don't entirely deny it. In a way, it's perfectly true. Now, don't get your hopes up, because I'm going to disappoint you. Have you noticed, Mr. Mitchell, that we rejoice in two parking places?"

"I hadn't."

"No reason why you should, since the other one is not at present in use. It's over there, at the mouth of the lane, under the trees. You can imagine what the Cove is like, in rainy weather; we drive all our cars over there, and squeeze them in. You'll probably see the tracks, if you look for them. The only trouble, apart from getting them out again, is that it's a sylvan spot, and simply crawling with wild life. Upholstery is sometimes gnawed by rodents, spiders drop down the backs of our necks, ants congregate in the mats. You can imagine."

He glanced up at Gamadge, who was listening with the tolerance of one who hears a mildly interesting tale, and glanced away again:

"My wife," he continued, "has implored me not to leave our poor old Ford out there all night. There it is." He waved benignly toward a battered antiquity, standing a few yards away, down the line. "A poor thing, but our only means of transport. But, being somewhat flustered by the preparations for our opening, I forgot it last night. However, I had been drinking a good deal of black coffee during the course of the evening, and I was not sleeping as soundly as usual. What I mean is," he added hastily, "I slept soundly, but I woke once or twice. The second time this happened, I remembered the car. I arose, crossed the clearing as quietly as possible, found my way as best I could through the fog, got into the bus, and propelled it as noiselessly as possible to the spot where it now stands. I knew better than to wake anybody up; really and truly, I believe our huskier young men would have murdered me, if I had. Does that solve your difficulty, Mr. Mitchell? I sincerely hope so."

Mitchell answered, woodenly: "You didn't need any light, for all this?"

"Oh, I can see in the dark. I even saw little Susie Baker, peering out from behind that tree, down there behind the trailer," said Atwood, in an airy tone.

"It's about as thin a story as I ever heard in my life."

"But it will serve, Mitchell, it will serve."

"I'll see you again. Don't go off this place."

"Why keep on repeating that injunction? Come up to the show, to-night; you will certainly see me, if you do. Before Callaghan gets through with me, I shall be in *all* the plays."

"I wouldn't miss it for worlds," Gamadge assured him. Atwood turned, stared into the impassive face so near his own, and said:

"On second thought, I do not include you in the invitation, my dear sir. You have the evil eye."

"That's unkind of you." Gamadge started the engine, and Atwood withdrew his arm and stepped back.

"Love to my relations, Sanderson," he said, "and all my sympathy. I'll be down to see them, when the law allows. Take good care of my aunt by marriage and my cousin Alma, won't you?"

The car started. He waved, and suddenly, as Gamadge grinned at him over a shoulder, extended the first and fourth fingers of his hand in a curiously ugly sign.

"What's he doing?" asked Sanderson, as they crossed the clearing.

"Oh—making the sign that's supposed to keep off the evil eye," said Gamadge.

"Why on earth has he got that idea about you?"

"Goodness knows. Perhaps he didn't like my suggesting that the gods were fixing to destroy him."

"Oh, *hubris*. I see. But do you think they are?"

"I'm not at all sure of it. Mr. Atwood wouldn't behave as he does if he weren't confoundedly satisfied with himself."

"He thinks he can get away with anything." Sanderson's expression was one of brooding anger. "Can't Mitchell do something or other?"

"Not without evidence; and that's the one and only thing Mr. Arthur Atwood isn't giving away."

"Curse the little brute." Sanderson gazed sombrely out of the window. "He's inhuman."

"Not really, you know," answered Gamadge. "That's all part of the performance."

CHAPTER NINE
Curious Interlude on the Golf Course

When they drew up at the Ocean House steps, Waldo ran out to them.

"Colonel Barclay's after you, Mr. Sanderson," he announced. "He wants you to come right down to the cottage."

"What for?"

"Mrs. Barclay and Fred Barclay are out somewheres, and the Colonel is having trouble with newspapers calling up. He wants help."

"Where the devil has Fred Barclay got to?"

"I don't know. The Colonel's been telephoning and telephoning."

"Blast it, I suppose I'd better go down." Waldo disappeared. Gamadge said, "I'll run you along there."

"But I can't desert like this. I'll have to see whether Mrs. Cowden——"

"I'm taking her and Miss Cowden out for a stroll on the golf course."

"No! That's splendid. I wish I could come along."

"I was going to suggest it, but I suppose you'd better see what the Colonel wants."

Gamadge made the trip to the Barclay cottage in four minutes. The Colonel received Sanderson with open arms, and made a valiant effort to detain Gamadge.

"These fellows are driving me out of my mind," he complained, "and I don't know what to say to them. Can't get hold of Ormville. You'll have to help me with something discreet—formula, you know."

"I'll do my best, sir. Less said the better I should think."

"If I had my way, I'd say nothing—hang up on 'em; but they tell me I mustn't do that."

"Oh, for God's sake, no. I'll handle it for you, Colonel."

The telephone rang madly from within the cottage.

"There they go again; New York's starting now," chattered the colonel. "The Ocean House is putting 'em all on me. My wife and Fred—don't know where they've got to."

"It's a shame, Colonel. I'll stand by."

Gamadge drove off to the frantic ringing of the telephone. He parked his car on the right of the hotel steps, and hurried in. Peabody sat on his bench near the desk.

"I'll be down in a minute," Gamadge told him. "Want you to do something for me. You, mind; not Waldo. That boy's always in too much of a hurry; attracts attention. This business requires tact."

"Yes, sir."

Gamadge climbed to his room, changed into golf clothes, and descended to the floor below. Hoskins sat at the doorway of Room 22, looking wizened in a porter's uniform much too big for him.

"Hello," said Gamadge. "Any callers?"

"Three. Tall, dark young feller came, just after you and Mitchell left. Looked at the sign on the door, and poked a piece of paper under before I could stop him."

"That was Lieutenant Barclay, I suppose."

"Whoever he was, he didn't like it much when I tapped him."

"Startle him, did you?"

"Well, he jumped."

"If you made Lieutenant Barclay jump, Hoskins, you performed something in the nature of a miracle."

"He made me so mad, pushin' that paper under the door, with that sign up sayin' not to disturb, that I fished it out again."

"You did?"

"Got down flat on my face, after he was gone, and slid it out with a foot rule I had in my pocket. I made a copy of it, and then I pushed it under again."

"I'm shocked at you. What did it say?"

"Here it is." Hoskins, looking at him owlishly, produced and handed over a folded sheet of Ocean House stationery. "Then," he went on, "a lady came up. Right after lunch. Pink dress, white hat, big knitting bag with wool flowers on it."

"That was Mrs. Barclay, Lieutenant Barclay's mother."

"She said she was Miss Cowden's aunt. She took a little bottle out of the bag, before she saw me, and went up to the door, and started to knock. When I sneaked up on her, she put the bottle back in a hurry."

"Aunt Julia's tonic, I suppose."

"She was mad as anything when I told her that sign meant business; but she went off quiet."

"Didn't try to see Mrs. Cowden?"

"No. Then the Colonel came, and he looked as though he was due for a stroke. Had a bunch of telegrams in his hand. Mrs. Cowden let him in, after I knocked and interduced him. He was quite polite about me," said Hoskins, looking surprised. "Said I was a good idea."

"Good for the Colonel."

"He told her he was glad they was goin' out with you to play golf, and they could get together after dinner and get busy on the correspondence. He left the telegrams, and went off. At four, Miss Cowden rang for her tea. Peabody brought it."

"Well, you're off duty for an hour, Hoskins."

"I feel like stayin' right here and havin' a nap."

"Do that. You'll need it. If you can manage it, I want you here till late to-night. After about 11:30 I'll take on myself, if necessary."

"I can stay right along, if you want me to."

"Good. We don't want Mrs. Barclay wandering in and trying to make Miss Cowden swallow that pick-me-up. Let's see what young Mr. Barclay has to say to his cousin Alma."

"I done right to copy it, didn't I?"

"That remains to be seen. If it's a private note of affectionate condolence, you did wrong. Very wrong." Gamadge went over to the north window of Room 22, and unfolded the paper. Hoskins watched him keenly. He read:

Thanks for the handout, but it's quite unnecessary, so far as I am concerned. Giving away money won't do you a bit of good. I want to see you, and you might as well make up your mind to it. Future proceedings depend entirely on you. It's in your hands.

Gamadge looked up at Hoskins, looked down at the note, and looked at Hoskins again. Then he said:

"You'll keep this to yourself."

"I certainly will. Ain't I the law?"

"That's the way to talk. I'm going down, now, to arrange a getaway for Mrs. Cowden and her niece. When Peabody comes up, co-operate with him."

"What's against the women goin' out for a walk?"

"Everything. They're supposed to be in seclusion. We don't want snapshots of them in the papers: 'Bereaved family play golf shortly after finding of body.' Who else has rooms on this floor, do you know?"

"Old lady and her daughter, Number 11, and Dr. and Mrs. Baines, 2 and 4, end of the corridor. More comin' in to-night from Canada and points south."

Mitchell, accompanied by a weedy individual in a pepper-and-salt suit who carried a briefcase, came to the door.

"We'll be obliged for your fingerprints," he said, "just in case you left any in 17."

The weedy individual got out his ink and pads, while Mitchell went and removed the seal from the door of 17. After being printed, Gamadge washed his hands in the bathroom of 22, and then hurried downstairs. He retired with Peabody to the alcove beside the coat closet.

"This is a delicate mission," he said. "Did Mrs. Cowden and Miss Cowden bring their golf clubs with them?"

"Yes, sir. They're in the closet."

"I want you to get a Number Five iron out of each of their bags."

"Some ladies don't have matched clubs, Mr. Gamadge."

"Mashie, then. Any sort of mashie. Watch your chance, and take them unobtrusively out by the back door, and around to the foot of the fire escape. Hide them under a bush or something. Then go up and knock at Room 21. Wait—post Hoskins down the hall, at the head of the stairs. Don't let the women come out of their rooms until the coast is clear. When they do come out, see them down the fire escape and give them their clubs."

Peabody nodded.

"Mrs. Cowden's been here before; she knows the back way to the tenth hole. I'll meet them on the tee."

Peabody asked no questions, but walked silently to the coat closet, and opened the door of it. Gamadge went out of the hotel by the back door, crossed the veranda, and descended to the square of short, rough grass that separated the Ocean House from the drive and the golf course. He turned right, and climbed a knoll to the golf club. This was a small building, which contained a lobby and locker rooms above, and the caddie master's precincts below. A shed, politely called the caddie house, seemed to be untenanted.

He went to his locker, got out his clubs, and then sought the caddie master. This official produced a very small caddie with sun-bleached hair under a ragged straw hat, and overalls rolled to his knees. He gazed timidly but hopefully at Gamadge, who murmured, "Oh, damn."

"Sorry, Mr. Gamadge, but he's the only one left." The caddie master also surveyed his underling without enthusiasm. "There's a match at Oakport—first of the season."

"Doesn't matter, only I have two ladies along, and we'll be held up, what with a threesome and lost balls."

"Good gosh, Mr. Gamadge, who's going to carry *their* clubs?"

"They're just walking around with mashies. What's your name, Caddie?... Norman? Come along. Wait a minute, though."

He pitched a niblick and two or three other irons out of his bag, the caddie master catching them as they fell. Norman slung the residue over his shoulder with a professional air, and waited, excitement mixed with apprehension in his eyes.

"Tenth tee," said Gamadge, "if you know where that is. I bet this is your first day out."

"Yes, but my brothers are caddies. I been around with them."

"All right, let's go."

Norman gamboling ahead, they followed the edge of the eighteenth fairway, crossed a bushy path, and skirted high shrubbery. Norman rushed along a plank walk that bridged the long, swampy rough; and Gamadge, climbing the tee, got three balls from the pocket of his bag.

Mrs. Cowden and her niece arrived as he fitted a wooden peg into the sandy soil. They both wore golf shoes. Mrs. Cowden carried a shining steel club, while Miss Cowden, detached and sombre, switched at the tall grasses with an ancient wooden mashie.

"Good for you," said Gamadge. "How was the getaway?"

"Perfectly managed. That charming little Peabody did it all as if he were managing an escape from the Bastille."

"Will you drive? I know you could use my clubs." He glanced with admiration at her long, well-muscled arms.

"Not yet, thanks. Perhaps I will try a shot, later on. I must steady down, first. Now, I should only drive into the swamp."

Gamadge violently waved Norman out of the middle distance, and drove. They walked up the deserted fairway, Miss Cowden slightly in the rear; she took an occasional chip shot, obviously not caring whether she hit the ball or not, while her aunt, hardly pausing in her long stride, sent her ball ahead in long, clean drives, and at last placed it faultlessly on the green.

"You don't need much steadying," Gamadge told her. "Here, take my putter."

Mrs. Cowden sank her ball in one. They went on to the next tee, Alma lingering behind with the tittering Norman, whose manners deteriorated as his self-possession grew. He looked on, vastly amused, while she knocked the ball aimlessly about the green.

"Alma plays pretty well, when she cares to be serious about it," said Mrs. Cowden. "Her clubs are shocking, of course; some old wooden ones of mine. Amberley was going to give her a new set for her birthday."

"If all her other ones have a warp in them like that mashie of hers, she'll end by being the best trick golfer in this part of the country."

"I'll tell you why I carry the good clubs, Mr. Gamadge—why I have carried them until now. After this, of course, Alma will have the best—of everything."

"That's good."

"I have not been able to provide the best for us both. Where golf is concerned, I have to play with women who play for money; and, other things being equal, steel clubs win. That is the sordid truth."

"Nothing sordid about it."

"You think not? Try counting the pennies for a few years, at your age, and see whether it isn't sordid."

"Your niece wouldn't allow you to count pennies, if she could help it; would she, Mrs. Cowden?"

"I don't think she would. Nor would Amberley have allowed it, if he had had an eye for pennies himself. He never thought of them."

Alma joined them on the next tee, and they played four holes without incident, except such as was supplied by Norman. He tripped and fell flat on his face, Gamadge's clubs spilling out of the bag on top of him; he had to have a nail removed from his shoe by Gamadge; he handed people brassies instead of drivers, and niblicks when they asked for putters; he stood in the middle of the greens to slap at mosquitoes, and took long drinks at all the fountains.

"This is a sporting shot," said Gamadge, as they climbed to the fifteenth tee. "You do it with an iron. Now, watch the balls, Norman," he begged. Norman galloped down to the green, and Gamadge chose a Number Four iron for Mrs. Cowden.

The fifteenth hole was a menace to players who sliced or hooked their drives. It was bounded on three sides by dense pinewoods; those on the right consisting of a thick belt which divided the fifteenth fairway from the sixteenth. The tee was very high, dipping sharply to a hollow behind, and overhanging a long, stony rough in front. Beyond the rough was a short, steep hill, and then a grassy slope to the green.

Mrs. Cowden said: "I remember this horror. A ball lost is a ball really lost."

Gamadge respectfully offered her his Four iron. She accepted it, and placed her ball on the green. Alma Cowden got a fine long shot with his Number Five, but it struck the side of the green, and bounded off into the underbrush on the left.

"Mark it, mark it," shouted Gamadge; but Norman had had no slightest idea of marking it; he had been taking his accustomed drink at the fountain. At the sound of Gamadge's voice he looked up guiltily, and then rushed over to the spot indicated by Gamadge, who stood pointing furiously with his iron. He began to scrabble in a hopeless and desultory fashion among the roots and dead leaves, while Gamadge placed his own ball on the green, not far from Mrs. Cowden's.

The three walked down from the tee, Alma well to the left, and leading. Norman scrabbled busily as they approached.

"Wretched boy," began Gamadge.

"Don't scold him; I think I know——" began Mrs. Cowden, and then the ball came past them. It just missed Alma Cowden's right ear, shot on and downwards, struck the trunk of a tree with the sound and, it almost seemed to them, the velocity of a bullet, and rebounded to Norman's feet.

Norman, not having seen it arrive, greeted its appearance with surprise and pleasure. Obviously hoping that he might be able to palm it off on them as the lost ball, he fell upon it, dug it from among the pine needles, and waved it triumphantly in the air.

Alma Cowden had stood still for a moment, immobilised by shock; afterwards she stared about her, as if vaguely aware that something had happened, she was not quite certain what. The others recovered themselves more quickly.

"Oh, God!" gasped Mrs. Cowden, actually staggering against Gamadge. She seized his arm, and he had to extricate it before he dashed back to the empty tee. Once there, he looked about him. No human being was in sight; long shadows lay across the turf, and the woods were dark and silent. A woodpecker resumed its tapping; somewhere, a crow cawed; and from the neighbouring fairway came the click of a golf ball. Gamadge, for the first time in his life, experienced a sense of the uncanny.

He came back to the green, and found the two women standing beside the drinking fountain, and Norman vigorously pumping water. The contrivance was one of those which shoot a small column vertically upwards, and Alma's face and the front of her blouse were drenched. Her aunt was offering a handkerchief. They were both deadly pale, Alma's pallor having the slight greenish tinge that betrays nausea.

"Did you…did you see anybody?" asked Mrs. Cowden.

"No. Fellow must have ducked, the minute he saw what had happened. He had plenty of time to make off before I got up there."

"How could it have been an accident? We were in plain sight."

"You think somebody tried to kill your niece with a golf ball?" Gamadge shook his head. "Won't do. A driver isn't a rifle, or even a catapult."

"Why did he run away?"

"Well, it's a public course; not all the people who use it are sportsmen, I suppose."

"Mr. Gamadge." She glanced behind her, to where Alma sat on a bench, drying her face and neck, while Norman hovered solicitously beside her. "You remember that Australian that used to play with Hagen, years ago?"

"Trick golfer; you mean him?" Gamadge regarded her curiously.

"Yes. He could do anything with a club and a ball. I've seen him—he could do anything. Mr. Gamadge, Arthur Atwood used to play like that. He didn't care for the game, and they said he cheated; but I saw him once——"

"Now, wait a minute."

"He can't miss, I tell you."

"But he did miss your niece, Mrs. Cowden; that is, if whoever it was took a shot at her. That's what I'm trying to tell you. He couldn't hope to be sure of it."

"But he could try."

"But golf is so chancy. If anything put him off his drive—that woodpecker up there, for instance; anything; or your niece turned her head——"

Young Barclay, a brassie under his arm, came around the trees on the right.

"Hello, there," he said, languidly.

"Hello," said Gamadge. "See any other solitary golfer come out of the woods in your vicinity?"

"No. Why?"

"Somebody just drove into us, and then vanished."

Lieutenant Barclay turned, looked up at the tee, and then back at his cousin.

"Alma seems to have been the victim," he said. "Did she get hit?"

"No. But it was a near thing."

"Funny. Probably some kid, if he ran for it." He went over to the bench, and pulled a large, immaculate handkerchief from his pocket. "Too bad, old girl," he said. "Tuck this in your collar."

Alma refused it with a shake of her head, rose, and moved away. She began to poke about in the pine needles for the lost ball, Norman at her heels. Fred Barclay stood, handkerchief in hand, looking at her. Gamadge turned back to Mrs. Cowden.

"What makes you all so afraid of that little man Atwood?" he asked.

"I'm not exactly afraid of him. I feel that he's the only person connected with us in any way who could possibly do such a thing."

"Serious allegation. Besides, he's up at the Cove—or ought to be. I can find out, perhaps."

Fred Barclay had lighted a cigarette, and stood leaning against a tree, quietly smoking. Alma shoved her mashie into Gamadge's bag, which Norman held for her, and said: "I can't find it."

"I think I can," said Mrs. Cowden. She went over to the spot, adding, with a certain grimness: "There's no reason why Mr. Gamadge should be victimised by our misfortunes. Where's that other ball, Caddie? You didn't find it, and you have no business pocketing it. Give it to me."

Norman, looking sheepish, produced it—a new ball, of excellent make. Gamadge came over to look at it.

"Interesting souvenir," he said. "I own several of that brand. Shall we present it to your niece? According to your theory, it's hers."

"I'd like you to take charge of it."

"Thanks." He dropped it into his pocket, and she began to rake efficiently under a root. Presently she extracted the ball, and handed it to him.

"Profound thanks." As Norman, stimulated by all this civility, retrieved the other ball from the green, he continued:

"That's right, put it in the bag, and put this one in, too. We've had enough golf for to-day. Don't look depressed; here's your fee, and here's your tip. Take the lady's club, stick it in my bag, and trot back to the caddie master with them; he'll keep them for me till I get a chance to put them in the locker."

"Will you take me out again?" Norman fingered his first earnings as if unable to believe his eyes.

"Certainly; do the whole eighteen. Now, be off with you."

Norman sped off by some short cut of his own. Young Barclay again approached his cousin.

"You look like the devil," he said. "Better hang on to my arm."

"Please let me alone, Fred."

Gamadge advanced, clasped her firmly by the elbow, and walked off with her down the next fairway. "Right back to the tenth," he said, "with the Ocean House in full view, and no stray balls coming from anywhere."

Young Barclay fell back beside Mrs. Cowden, casting a long, slow, coldly furious look at Gamadge; for which the latter hardly blamed him.

"What you want," he said, "is a good stiff drink, Miss Cowden. The time for sedatives is past; the time for stimulants has come. How about a stiff one in Room 22—just you and Hoskins and I? There's some good Scotch in my suitcase."

"I'd like a drink," confessed Miss Cowden.

"You don't want Fred along?"

"I'd rather not," she replied, staring in front of her.

"All right, we won't have him. He's annoyed with me at the moment, anyway; he might cast a gloom. Will your aunt insist upon joining us? Not that we don't want her, of course, but what I say is, let us occasionally relax outside the family circle. Hoskins is going to be on the job, to-night, by the way."

"Is he?"

"Yes, I'm going up to the Cove, to see this show; I'll be back by 11.30, at the latest, I should think. I was there this afternoon, and met Mr. Atwood. He tells me I have the evil eye."

She gave him a quick, wondering glance.

"I also met your brother's friend, little Miss Baker. Susie Baker. Do you know her?"

"No, I don't. I've heard him speak of her."

"Nice little thing. Was he fond of her?"

"I don't know. We didn't see very much of each other, Mr. Gamadge. He didn't tell me anything. He was away a good deal, with his tutors. In a way, I hardly knew him. We led such entirely different lives."

"And of course you were younger."

"I was always at school."

"Excuse me for asking these personal questions; did he give you an allowance?"

"He gave me presents. Amby needed almost all his money for himself, he really did. Doctors, and treatments. And cruises."

"I can see that." Gamadge wished that he could control a perpetual impulse to glance behind him. They were well out in the middle of the fairway, and beyond danger from any driven ball; but he found himself looking over his shoulder just the same. He went on: "Hoskins says your aunt, Mrs. Barclay, came along with some sort of physic for you. Does she fancy herself as a pharmacist?"

"She's always trying to doctor people. She used to have a medicine chest, when she and Uncle Harrison were in the Army."

"For God's sake, don't let her go putting any of her brews into your stomach. Pour them down the drain, and tell her they did you a world of good."

The distant click of a golf ball made them both jump. Alma Cowden looked at him with a faint smile. "I wonder if that sound will always make me duck, after this," she said.

"Don't think too much about the incident. Somebody on the tee, practising; 'Never thought he could shoot as far as that'; I've heard the story before, and so have you."

She gave him a straight look. "You couldn't find him."

"I didn't try; hopeless job, with all that cover. Your cousin was probably right; some young ass, who cut in from the road without bothering to go up to the club and pay his fees. He's in the next township by now, unless I'm very much mistaken, selling his clubs."

"You know very well that he was trying to hit me, Mr. Gamadge."

"Who was?"

"I don't know."

"You know as well as I do that nobody on that tee could hope to hit anything smaller than the green."

"Arthur Atwood——"

"Now don't give me any of that Atwood stuff! Let's eliminate him. He's up at the Cove, with a state cop on the premises, and strict orders to stay there."

"Couldn't he get out through the woods, and get a lift somewhere along the road?"

"Bother it, perhaps he could; I should have thought nothing bigger than a chipmunk could navigate that brush. Forget him; I'll find out whether he left the place."

"Did you find out whether he left there last night?" She looked up at him, her lips set.

"Had me there. Look here, Miss Cowden; you're mighty anxious to pin this on Atwood, and so is your aunt. As a matter of fact——"

They had now reached the tall bushes that concealed the tenth tee. The sharp crack of a golf ball brought them to a momentary halt; they smiled grimly at each other, and rounded the screen of willows. Mrs. Barclay stood alone on the tee, driver in one hand, the other shading her eyes against the blazing afternoon sun.

CHAPTER TEN
Gamadge Cultivates Poise

Mrs. Barclay was too much absorbed to notice her audience. She removed her hand from her eyes, sought vainly about her feet for her wooden tee, removed another from her hatband, and pushed it firmly into the earth. She then placed a grimy ball upon it, straightened, grasped her driver, and raised it. Her long arms in their tight pink sleeves descended in a magnificent follow through, and the ball shot grandly over the rough and landed well up in the middle of the fairway.

Gamadge applauded, and so, after a pause, did Alma Cowden.

Mrs. Barclay turned, and regarded them benignantly. "That was a lucky one," she said.

"More management than luck, Mrs. Barclay. I congratulate you."

"My short game is very poor, as you know. How nice that you feel able to be out, Alma; but is it wise? You look exhausted."

"Miss Cowden nearly had an accident," said Gamadge.

"Oh, dear; your aunt Eleanor won't like to hear that. Did she approve of your coming out?"

Mrs. Cowden answered the question by coming around the bushes with Lieutenant Barclay. His mother stared.

"Well!" she exclaimed. "You out too, Eleanor!"

"Yes, Lulu, as you see, I am out," replied Mrs. Cowden, calmly. "So are you; so is Fred; and so, I am glad to see, is poor Hugh Sanderson."

That young man could indeed be descried in the distance, putting on the eighteenth green.

"Only Dad missing," said young Barclay. "He must be at the beach, by this time. Shall we go down, Mum, or are you finishing this hole? You'll do it in par, if you keep up; you've made a better start at it than I generally do."

"I'll come with you, dear. Will you get my balls?"

"Leave them for the caddies; they look like mushrooms. You deserve new ones, after those drives."

"I have a box of lovely new ones that I won at bridge, but I never use them on this awful tee. Once in the marsh, and they're gone."

"Mum makes her own golf rules," observed Fred, dropping his brassie into her bag, and shouldering it. "Changing balls in mid-game is O.K. with her."

"I wouldn't do it in a match, Freddy."

"Not if your partner knew it, you wouldn't." He went down the other side of the tee, refraining from any glance in the direction of his cousin or Gamadge. Mrs. Barclay lingered to say:

"What's this I hear about Alma having an accident, Eleanor?"

"Somebody drove into us on the fifteenth."

"Oh, dear! Who?"

"We couldn't find out."

"How dreadful. Who could it have been, Freddy?"

"Didn't see the outrage. A caddie, perhaps. They practise when they get a chance."

"I hope you will report it at the club. The course is positively dangerous, nowadays, with all these people from the small hotels crowding in."

"Now, Mum, you know you hit old Macpherson in the ankle, and how nice he was about it. Come along, if you want a swim before supper."

"I'll see you this evening, Eleanor."

They went off, and the Cowdens and Gamadge returned to the Ocean House by the back way. A big young man in a porter's uniform watched them with interest as they all climbed the fire-escape stairs, and then went on loading baggage on the freight elevator.

Doctor and Mrs. Baines were just arriving at the door of Number 21 when the three surprised them by a flank movement from the left; the doctor vast, calm and benign, his wife also large, also serene, and full of cheerful solicitude. They were delighted to hear that there had been a walk, and puzzled as well as horrified by the story of the mysterious golf ball. Gamadge brought forward his idea (slightly edited) of the orgy in Room 22, but the doctor vetoed it.

"Won't do, young man," said Baines. "Won't do at all. I know a trick worth two of that. Meanwhile, the patient would be all the better for a short period of rest and relaxation before her dinner."

Alma disappeared, and he went on:

"I don't much like her colour, and there are signs of shock. Less hysterical, though; much less hysterical. Not your fault that the cure wasn't entirely a success, Gamadge."

"Thanks. Look here, I'm going to have a drink before I go down to the beach; let me bring my stuff down here. There's plenty for all, and Mrs. Cowden could do with a stiff one, or I'm much mistaken."

"Much obliged to you, but we had our afternoon maximum dose a few minutes ago."

"And we needed it; the sea is dreadfully cold, to-day," said Mrs. Baines.

"Have to bear up now until dinner-time; won't we, Molly? My wife and I are great believers in rum old-fashioneds, and the barman here—what's his name—Murphy—makes them very well. I'll have them send you up one, Ellie; no liquor for the little girl, though."

Gamadge said: "Sorry my diagnosis was wrong. How about you, Mrs. Cowden? Care for a highball?"

"I should be only too glad of one."

He went up to his room, got out the remains of a bottle of whisky, and sent for a jug of ice and glasses. When he returned to Number 21 with the tray, Doctor Baines and his wife had gone. Sanderson joined him at the door.

"Well, Hugh; you look very hot and tired." Mrs. Cowden accepted her glass from Gamadge with gratitude. “What a pet Bertie Baines is; don’t you think so, Mr. Gamadge?”

“Rather a formidable pet.” He handed Sanderson the other glass, and mixed a drink for himself in one which Mrs. Cowden brought from the bathroom. “He’s a holy terror in medical jurisprudence, and no jury has ever brought in a verdict against his evidence.”

“I knew he had a wonderful reputation. I hope you two are going down for a swim.”

“I’d like nothing better. You going, Gamadge?” asked Sanderson.

“I certainly am.”

“Gosh, this is what I needed! You’re a Samaritan, old man.” Sanderson drained his glass, and then took a sheet of paper out of his wallet, and handed it to Mrs. Cowden. “Here’s the statement the Colonel and I drew up for the Press. We called up the sheriff, and he approved. I only hope you will.”

She read it, and passed it to Gamadge. “It will do, I suppose. Very clever of you, Hugh,” she said, wearily.

“Did they like it?” Gamadge handed it back. It was short, and had a disarming effect of candour: Amberley Cowden had left the hotel shortly after his arrival with his family; he had expressed interest in the aspect of the “sea turn,” and had probably strolled down the road, and climbed to the top of the cliff, to get the full effect of it. The cliff was only a couple of minutes’ walk from the hotel, and the climb to it was short and easy. Unfortunately, the boy had an advanced case of myocarditis, and this last exertion had proved too much for him. Doctors Cogswell and Baines were mentioned by name, as were also the Barclays. No reference, of course, was made to money, birthdays, the Atwoods or Seal Cove.

“They had to like it. We gave it out to five papers, local and otherwise, and to the Associated Press. Then we quit. The Colonel went down for a swim, and I got in a little putting.”

“We saw you,” said Mrs. Cowden.

“Did you get out? Splendid.”

“Very splendid. I went against my better judgment, and when I do that I always regret it. Now you two must go down and get your bathe. The Barclays are coming up after dinner, so you’re off for the rest of the day, Hugh. You’ve done your share, until to-morrow.”

“That’s awfully good of you; I should like to turn in early. Come along to my room, Gamadge, will you, while I get my bathing suit?”

Room 20 was small and hot; it contained a washbasin equipped with gurgling water pipes, and, judging from the clash of crockery that came in through its uncurtained window, it was directly over the kitchen. Sanderson apologised for its disorder.

“I’m not even unpacked yet,” he said, removing clothes and books from the bed, so that Gamadge could sit down. A suitcase stood on the only chair, and he proceeded to rummage in it. He dragged out a bathing suit, added a raincoat to it, and said he was ready.

"A raincoat's a great help," he remarked, slamming the door behind them. "Beach robe, dressing gown, what you please. Look here, Gamadge; what did Mrs. Cowden mean, about regretting her walk with you?"

"Somebody was taking pot shots at Miss Cowden on the golf course."

"What!" Sanderson stopped, and stared at him.

"Golf ball nearly hit her. Come on, I'll tell you about it after we get outside."

When they were on their way down the drive, Gamadge described the incident. Sanderson looked bewildered. "I never heard of anything like it," he said. "Do you mean it was an accident?"

"Well, the women think not. Of course, the fellow must have run like a rabbit, afterwards."

"It couldn't possibly have been a stray ball from another tee? Or another fairway?"

"You don't know the terrain, or you wouldn't ask that."

"It couldn't have been done on purpose." Sanderson looked frightened.

"I don't quite know how to explain myself, but there was something exceedingly purposeful about the way it came shooting down."

"But, good Lord! It *must* have been an accident."

"That's what Fred Barclay says."

"Was he with you?"

"Playing on the next fairway. He joined us afterwards. He was playing alone."

Gamadge put no particular significance into his tone, but Sanderson looked at him sharply.

"And Mrs. Barclay was on the tenth tee, also playing alone," said Gamadge.

"And I was on the eighteenth green also playing alone. Don't talk rot," begged Sanderson.

"I'm just giving you the general picture."

"Mrs. Barclay!"

"Good player, Mrs. Barclay, until she gets up to the green."

"How—how is Alma taking it?"

"Very well. A little upset, naturally, but Baines has seen her, and I think she'll be all right."

"What does she think about it? What does her aunt think?"

"Well, they seem to be more or less obsessed by the idea of our friend Atwood."

"Atwood? Nonsense. He's sewed up there at the Cove."

"He is, if mortal man can sew Atwood up. I'm going up there to the show, as you remember; so's Mitchell. We'll have to try and find out whether he was on hand this afternoon."

"They have this unreasonable horror of the fellow. I suppose he must have been an uncanny sort of boy."

"Curious phenomenon in a respectable family. His mother was Mrs. Barclay's sister, wasn't she?"

"Yes, the eldest of three. I gather that she was more or less the family fool. She was in her late forties when she eloped with Atwood; some sort of vaudeville actor. You can imagine the scandal."

"I suppose the family never saw much of the son."

"On the contrary, they tried to give him a lift when the parents died, which they did when he was only a kid. Hopeless proposition—there was no holding him. When he was old enough, he went on the stage himself, and married there. This woman is his third wife. Poor old Amby never knew him at all, or hardly. Thought he was a romantic figure. All that nonsense of Atwood's tickled him—and, of course, he did rather like the idea of being a patron. It gave him an interest. Nice feelings, he had; always out for the underdogs—such as myself." He smiled. "That's the way he thought of me."

They had reached the bathhouse, where they separated; Sanderson to engage a cabin, Gamadge to seize two towels from the shelf, and disappear into his own cubicle. He got into his bathing suit, and ran across the beach to the edge of the water. It was almost as quiet as a pond; pale blue and twinkling in the distance, glassy green inshore. Thin ruffles of surf broke at his feet.

He shuddered, knowing the signs; this was going to be an icy dip. He dashed in, plunged, and came up gasping. After a swim just long enough to prove that he wasn't afraid of cold water, he waded out, flung his bathrobe over his shoulders, and went along the narrow plank walk towards the nearest gap in the sea wall. His way took him past the Barclays, who were assembled in a family group; Mrs. Barclay and the Colonel in deck chairs, their son at their feet, his hands clasped about his shins and a sweater tied by its sleeves around his neck. Like a contemplative god, he sat gazing beyond the shouting children and the striped umbrellas, out to sea.

Mrs. Barclay gave the shivering young man who addressed her a cool reception. "Fred's told on me," thought Gamadge, and said to the god below him: "Mitchell and I are driving up to the Cove, to-night. Want to come along?"

"Are you asking me?" Young Barclay turned his head and looked up.

"Yes."

"No, thanks; there's been a death in the family."

Gamadge said, amiably: "The trip was to be in the nature of business."

Colonel Barclay, who had apparently been dozing, opened his eyes. "Part of this sheriff's investigation?" he asked.

"Yes; sir. Not only that; there's been a death up there—one of the actresses. Mitchell's looking into it."

"God bless me! Another inquest?"

"Another inquest."

The Colonel said: "I never heard anything like it. What's this I hear about Alma being hit by a golf ball?"

"She wasn't hit, sir."

"If she had been, she would have been killed; outrageous. I understand you couldn't find the scoundrel."

Lieutenant Barclay observed, in a dispassionate tone: "What I can't quite make out is why you didn't look around a bit. I gather that you never even left the tee."

"Well, no, I didn't," replied Gamadge, still more amiably. "I figured that there were three fairways within a few yards, just beyond that belt of pines up there. If I had gone through, and met a lone golfer on any one of them, innocently knocking his ball about; would it have done much good to have asked him politely if he had just failed to commit a homicide?"

Colonel Barclay said, irritably: "Not so much criticism, Fred. Gamadge and Sanderson have been doing their best all day to help us out of our difficulties. I can't say as much for you. You took yourself off, this afternoon——"

"Now, Father!" protested Mrs. Barclay.

The choleric blue eyes wandered seaward. "There's going to be another sea turn, to-night," said the Colonel.

"No; really?" Gamadge, in turn, looked out over the dazzling ocean, and up at the clear blue sky.

"Land breeze is dead, air's softening, not a cloud up there, and you can see the haze on the horizon."

"So I can." The white line between sea and sky was indeed broader than it had been. "Well, my teeth are beginning to chatter. I'd better get my clothes on."

He went up to the bathhouse. When he came out, Sanderson joined him, looking half-frozen, the damp and sandy raincoat bunched over his arm.

"My heavens," he said, "what water! Is it always like that?"

"Always, when there's a land breeze." They walked up the road, Gamadge rather wishing that he was alone. He wanted time to sort out the jumble of his ideas. "Evidence, evidence, evidence," he brooded, while Sanderson's chat sounded in his ears. "We haven't a scrap of it that would stand up for one instant in a court of law. And yet I *know*. Maddening…What's that you say?"

"I said, 'What kind of ball was it?'"

"Dreadnought 3. I use them, everybody uses them. Mrs. Barclay uses them—up."

"Do stop talking about Mrs. Barclay! It's too grotesque."

"I shouldn't care to have her drive into me, I can tell you…" He retired again into his thoughts: "What's the use of telling Mitchell? He'd only take action, and ruin everything. I can't tell him yet. I don't dare. Evidence. If I could only…"

They went up the Ocean House steps, and into the lobby. New arrivals were at the desk, where Wilks, the freckled day clerk, presided fussily. He saw Gamadge, and waved to him. "Telegrams for you, sir."

Gamadge had stopped dead in his tracks, his thoughts racing. "Great Caesar's ghost! What did—wait a minute. I must cultivate poise. That's it; nerves of steel, like Fred Barclay. Like Mitchell."

Sanderson looked at him, wonderingly. "What's the matter?" he asked.

"Something I just remembered. My telegrams. Forgot all about them."

They went up to the desk, and Wilks handed two yellow envelopes to Gamadge, and some letters to Sanderson. "You were on the golf course when these came, sir," he said to Gamadge. "At least, so Peabody told me. I didn't think they were urgent, so I didn't chase you." Wilks, having taken them himself over the telephone, saw no reason why he should pretend ignorance of their contents.

"Thanks. No, I don't suppose they are."

"Just day letters, about that club you were thinking of joining."

"Club? Oh, yes." Gamadge wished that his fingers had not such an irresistible tendency to jerk at the envelopes as he opened them. He glanced casually about him; up at the clock, right and left at the arrivals and their luggage, down at the register beneath his nose. "Has Miss Macpherson come?" he asked. "No, I see she hasn't. She'd better; her uncle's arranged a foursome for tomorrow."

"Coming to-night, sir, on the C.P.R."

"Golf champion?" enquired Sanderson.

"Could be, if she wasn't a trained nurse. People are coming in, Wilks; we won't know the place in a day or so. You ought to see it at the top of the season," he told Sanderson. "Especially on a rainy night. All the cottage people stay in the place and play bridge. Children dashing around and yelling, radio going, tobacco smoke so thick you could cut it, card tables jammed together like sardines, and half a dozen Mah Jong die-hards rattling tiles in one corner."

"I'm afraid I shall miss all that," said Sanderson, rather wistfully.

Wilks coughed. "We hate to lose your party, sir. Four rooms and two baths. But we wouldn't hold you, not even for a week, after such a tragedy."

Gamadge spread his day letters out on the desk, planted his elbows one on either side of them, and read them through, "All right so far," he reflected. "Poise, perfect poise."

"Very decent of you," Sanderson was telling Wilks. "Mrs. Cowden appreciates it."

Gamadge read the letters through a second time. Then he put them in his pocket, nodded to Sanderson, and drifted away. He walked up the stairs quietly enough, but when he reached his own room, his demeanour altered. He whistled piercingly as he changed into tweeds, brushed his hair, and put on brown shoes. Then he glanced out of the window at the pearly haze which had now risen high above the horizon, seized a topcoat and a soft hat, and ran down three flights of stairs to the café in the basement.

CHAPTER ELEVEN
Danger

Mitchell sat waiting for him at a small table between the window and the door. Several people stood at the bar counter, Doctor and Mrs. Baines among them; but no other table was occupied. Gamadge asked: "Have you searched the Cowden car yet?"

"Yes. Not a thing in it but road maps and Sanderson's driving licence, and a squashed packet of cigarettes."

"Who has the keys?"

"I just sent 'em up to Sanderson. How's Miss Cowden, after her accident?"

"You heard about that, did you?"

"It's all over the beach. I understand the story came from the caddie house."

"I wasn't sure that Norman had taken it in; at the time, he seemed more or less to accept it as part of the hazards of the game."

"Your caddie, was he?"

"He was engaged as a caddie—Class X, I should say. I haven't seen Miss Cowden since we got home. She was considerably upset just after it happened, but she's had a visit from Baines, and I dare say she's better. Look here, Mitchell; could you put a man on the Cowden car for the rest of the night?"

"Put a man on it?"

Gamadge had remained standing. He now ordered an old-fashioned from the waiter, and asked Mitchell if he wanted a drink.

"Don't use 'em, thanks."

"Then we'll just have two suppers. Two suppers, Mickey. There isn't any choice down here in the grill, you know, Mitchell; we take what they give us, and it's always good."

"Anything suits me. What do you mean," enquired Mitchell again, when Mickey had gone, "putting a man on the Cowden car?"

Gamadge sat down and leaned forward. "It's this way: that car might very well have to go out to-night on an errand. I'd feel very much happier if I knew a state policeman would trail it, on a motorcycle."

Mitchell, greatly puzzled, stared at him for some time in silence. Then he said: "That business on the golf course got you scared, did it?"

"I was considerably scared."

"But if Mrs. Cowden sent the car out, Sanderson would be driving it; and he probably wouldn't be going any further than Oakport, if she wanted something from the drug store."

"Oakport would be much too far for Mr. Sanderson to drive alone."

"You think even *Sanderson's* in some kind of danger?"

"I'm convinced he is."

"I could get hold of a man, but I'd have to have a good reason for giving him the job. I have two fellers already up at the Cove."

"I'll give you the reason as soon as I'm sure of it myself. If you can't put the trooper on, I'll have to stay at home and do it myself, and I don't know how."

Mitchell, still gazing at him doubtfully, rose slowly from his chair.

"When you come back, I have some telegrams to show you," said Gamadge. "Harold has done his best to justify his existence."

Mitchell went out, and was gone until Gamadge had finished his old-fashioned, and the waiter had brought clam chowders. Nothing was said until these had been sampled; Mitchell then glanced about the café, convinced himself that he could not be overheard by the occupants of the nearest table (who happened to be the Baineses), and said grumblingly:

"I got hold of Loomis. He's going down to the garage now. I don't suppose there's any reason for him keeping under cover?"

"None at all, if you don't object to making Sanderson nervous. There may be nothing in my little notion, you know; shame to get the wind up these people unnecessarily."

"It's getting so foggy, Loomis might miss him if he didn't stick pretty close."

"Well, I'm greatly obliged to you. Here are Harold's communications; as I told you, he revels in the cryptic; I couldn't imagine what Wilks meant, when he talked about a club."

Mitchell read the day letters while the clam chowder bowls were removed and the hot boiled lobster substituted. They ran as follows:

GAMADGE, OCEAN HOUSE, FORD'S BEACH, MAINE

CALLED UP WELLS GRUBY MISS CADWALLADER ABOUT CLUB YOU ARE INTERESTED IN ALSO SAW TOWN TALK THOMPSON AND BACK FILES PUBLIC LIBRARY ALL AGREE IT IS OLD WELLKNOWN SOCIAL CONCERN BUT SLIPPING FINANCIALLY SINCE NINETEEN FOURTEEN EXCEPT PARIS BRANCH WHICH CLOSED DOWN YEARS AGO STOP MEMBERS HIGH-TONED MORE COMING LATER

H. BANTZ

GAMADGE, FORD'S BEACH

SAW BIGGS AND CAROLINE CADE RE CLUB MEMBERSHIP NO PUBLICITY NO SCANDALS SINCE NINETEEN EIGHT WHEN MEMBER ELOPED WITH ACTOR SHE WAS THROWN OUT OF CLUB AND SOCIAL REGISTER HER SON NOT ELIGIBLE WELL-KNOWN ON SMALL TIME AS FEMALE IMPERSONATOR MARRIED FLORENCE FALLS MORE COMING

H. BANTZ

"My, my." Mitchell folded the telegrams, and handed them back. "I don't know how I can wait for the rest of it."

"You don't sound as if you found Harold's researches interesting."

"They don't tell us much we didn't know, do they?"

"The little more, and how much it is. Any objection to Hoskins spending the night in Room 22?"

"No, but the sheriff may not want to pay his bill."

"I'll see that it's paid."

"Since he's here as the Cowdens' bodyguard, they ought to pay it."

"Perhaps they will. How did the fingerprinting come out?"

"Amberley Cowden's were all over the fittings in the dressing case. There wasn't another print in the room, except yours and mine."

"You don't say!"

"That tells a story, don't it? Looks as if somebody got into that room ahead of us, and did considerable wiping up afterwards."

"Or wore gloves."

"The boy may never have taken his off; they were on when Sam saw him. These French fried potatoes go pretty good with the lobster, don't they?"

Gamadge nodded, with his mouth full. He took a swallow of coffee, and said: "The will wasn't in the dressing case, then."

"I bet anything he had it on him."

They had reached the asparagus course when Doctor Baines came across the room, flapped them back into their seats with a large hand, and sat down at the table. He rumbled:

"Sorry to interrupt you; I'm going back to my own dessert in a minute. They had me back at that mortuary of yours, Mitchell, to look at the actress."

"So I heard, Doctor; we appreciate it."

"Your man Cogswell's a very good man, and all I did was corroborate his findings. Those pills were quarter-grain morphia tablets, and you'll find she took enough to kill her. Not much doubt that she died of an overdose of morphia. There was an abscessed tooth. We can't seem to find out who prescribed. May have to advertise."

"So I hear."

"She was dead by two this morning, and so was the boy. He died of his myocarditis, just as we all knew he would. You going to keep his family up here, till you find out why he climbed up on that cliff?"

"We don't want to put them to unnecessary trouble."

"They ought to get away from the place. I suppose the money situation bothers you."

"He did die right quick after he got it."

"He did."

"And I understand that somebody tried to kill his sister right after she got it," said Mitchell, calmly eating asparagus.

"I am inclined to diagnose that case as accident." Baines glanced at Gamadge, and went on: "I have been acquainted with the hazards of this golf course for thirty years. There are three people who might conceivably be supposed to have a motive for assassinating little Alma Cowden: the elder Barclays, her cousin Fred Barclay, and her other cousin, Arthur Atwood. He's an extravert, and he used to be an egomaniac; I never heard that he was an out-and-out damned fool. Lulu Barclay's a silly woman, and she's spoiled young Fred; I shouldn't have thought there was any harm in either of 'em. These people are having their lawyer up, you know."

"So I heard."

Mickey took away the asparagus, and brought strawberries. Baines waited until he left, and then went on:

"Ormville's a sound man, high reputation, big family practice; I doubt if he could handle this situation. I've known Harrison Barclay all my life, and I'm fond of the old fool. Shall I get hold of a first-rate criminal lawyer for him? Get him up here for the inquest?"

"No need to worry about it just yet, Doctor. I'll keep you posted."

Baines lumbered to his feet. "I'm going over tomorrow, as a friend of the family."

"Glad to have you."

"What's your standing in this business?" Baines turned abruptly to Gamadge, who answered blandly:

"The same as yours, Doctor, if I may say so without impertinence. I've been called in unofficially—as an expert."

"Oh." He went back to his table, and Mitchell said:

"That reminds me; when are you going to do some expert work on that ink? To-morrow morning?"

"Delighted; if you still want me to. We'd better be on our way, I think. It's going to be a foggy trip. Meet you in the lobby in ten minutes."

The atmosphere of Room 22 was peaceful. Hoskins' collar was off, and he was in his shirtsleeves. He sat devouring a substantial-looking dinner, his table being so placed that he could see Mrs. Cowden's door, and seven-eighths of Miss Cowden's.

"Where's your disguise?" asked Gamadge.

"They took it back again. I guess the other porter must have come; I hear there's a lot of folks checking in to-night."

"You don't need it. Keep awake, now; send down for more coffee, if you need it. I'll be back before 11:30, I should think."

"I ain't sleepy," protested Hoskins. "Had a nice nap."

"We heard you having it."

"When?"

"When we came in from golf. Heard you snoring like mad, through the transom."

"Well, I had to keep it open. These land-side rooms are awful hot."

"A corner one shouldn't be."

"What's that state trooper doin' down at the garage?"

"Watching over you. See you later."

As he passed Room 19 on his way down the corridor to the stairs, he heard a low voice call him by name. He stopped, and turned.

"Hello," he said, just above a whisper.

"Hello. Will you come in a minute?"

"What did you say?"

"I said, please come in." The crack in the door widened.

Gamadge cast a hunted look up and down the corridor; Hoskins was eyeing him, with apparent detachment, over the rim of a coffee cup; otherwise there was no one in sight. Gamadge slipped through the doorway. Miss Alma Cowden stood just within, a neat dark-blue tailored dressing gown over her dark-blue pyjamas; they looked at each other, while Gamadge put a hand behind him and closed the door.

"I had to see you," she told him.

"Well; trouble is, these business conferences in hotel bedrooms are so apt to leak out. It's almost a law. Would your aunt care for this?"

"She can't hear. She's lying down, and both the bathroom doors are shut. I locked them, too."

"That makes it perfect."

"And nobody will come except Waldo or Peabody, with my dinner tray. They wouldn't say anything."

"But how embarrassing for you, to have Waldo or Peabody going around not saying anything."

"I can't help it. I couldn't wait. Mr. Gamadge," she turned a pale, determined face up to him, "I've changed my mind about that money. I'm not going to give those legacies to those people."

"Oh; aren't you, though?"

"No, I'm not."

"Want me to go around telling them so?"

"No, I can let them know later. Mr. Gamadge, I'm not going to keep any of that money."

Gamadge studied her face, keeping his own blank. At last he said: "You mean the million you're getting from your brother's estate?"

"Yes. How can I give it all away?"

"But, *querida di mi alma!* That's a fearful lot of money to toss out of the window. What's your reason?" As she did not answer, he went on: "Plenty of good ones, of course; let's see; do you want to marry some young man who won't have a rich wife? Nonsense. You can persuade him to let you keep it; just work on him a little. Or perhaps you're thinking of going into a nunnery; don't do it, you're not the type." She said nothing, and he went on after a moment: "Or are you still brooding about that golf ball? Still afraid somebody's going to bump you off? I should say they would be much more likely to do it, if they knew you were planning to give all the money away. Why don't you keep them guessing till you're of age?"

She said in a violent whisper: "Of age! Of age! I feel as if I had never heard anything but that in all my life. I hate the sound of the words. Can't I sign something, and give the money away now?"

Gamadge, looking at her, hesitated. Then he said: "It might be arranged."

Her face cleared, "I was afraid I couldn't."

"Well. All things considered—look here. I can draw up a paper for you, and Hoskins and I can witness it. But, my dear good child, have you really thought it over? A million dollars!"

"I won't touch that money, Mr. Gamadge."

"Can't you tell me why not?"

"No."

Gamadge had become very grave. He glanced about the small, narrow room, neatly arranged for the night; at the turned-down bed, the little table beside it with its pink-shaded lamp, the chintz curtains. Then, looking her firmly in the eye, he said: "Your brother died a natural death, you know. Baines says so."

"Yes, I know."

"Your people won't like this. Suppose they cut off supplies?"

"I have a little money of my own."

"You won't sleep on this very serious business matter?"

"I want to get it settled. I can't sleep unless I do."

"Let's go, then." Gamadge, after a nervous glance at the communicating door, sat down at her writing table and got out his fountain pen. "Any particular person you want to give it to?" he asked, looking up at her.

"No, I don't know of anybody. I suppose…" She frowned, hesitated, and said again: "No."

"All right. You just renounce all claim to it, and leave it to be scrambled for. And believe me, there'll be some scrambling." Gamadge reflected, wrote, reflected again, and wrote hurriedly. "How's this?" he asked finally, and read from the sheet of Ocean House letter paper:

"TO WHOM IT MAY CONCERN

I, Alma Cowden, hereby renounce all claim to my brother Amberley Cowden's estate, and solemnly declare this to be my irrevocable intention. I clearly understand that this document is legal and binding, and it is signed by me in the presence of two witnesses."

Alma also looked grave. "It sounds right," she said judicially. "It's just what I wanted."

"I'll get Hoskins."

He slid out of the room, summoned Hoskins with a crooked finger, and pushed him through the doorway of Room 19. He then explained in a whisper that Miss Cowden wanted her signature witnessed.

Hoskins took the paper, read it twice, and looked fishily up at Gamadge. "You crazy?" he asked, in a loud whisper.

"No. Ssh. Sign, Miss Cowden."

She did so. Gamadge signed, and then handed the pen to Hoskins, who received it automatically, still fixing Gamadge with a glassy stare.

"Go ahead and sign." Gamadge nudged him sharply.

Hoskins sat down at the table, read the paper again, tugged at the collar of his shirt, and laboriously traced a large "Willard G. Hoskins, Deputy Sheriff," under Gamadge's signature. He then rose, and allowed himself to be firmly pushed out into the corridor. Gamadge closed the door, and folded the paper. He asked:

"Do you want me to turn this over to that lawyer of yours, when he comes?"

"I suppose so."

"He'll go up in the air."

"Perhaps he will, but I always liked Mr. Ormville."

"Well, we'll hope for the best. Think you can stall him off as easily as you do me, when he starts asking questions?"

"Yes, I do."

"That's all settled, then. Now, remember: no jitters to-night. Hoskins will be right there till morning. Sleep well."

"Thank you for everything, Mr. Gamadge. It's funny; I haven't anybody but you."

"That is accidental, and purely temporary. Good night."

"Good night."

He went out, heard the key turn in the lock of her door, and faced Hoskins. The latter seized him, and drew him into Room 22.

"See here," he demanded sternly. "What you up to? She can't convey any property. She's a minor."

"She can do anything she wants to. Let the lawyer tear the thing up, if he likes; she'll get a good night's sleep out of it, anyhow."

He dashed downstairs, and found Mitchell on the veranda, looking out on a dream world. Everything but the nearest trees and bushes had been blotted out by a white wall of fog, through which the light on the driveway showed palely, like a wet moon.

"Careful, now," begged Mitchell, when they were in Gamadge's car.

"You telling me?" Gamadge slowly manœuvred his way around the sweep and down the drive.

"Of course we'll go by the state road. It'll make us late. Do you think those actors will try to give the show?"

"If I know the profession, they'll give it for just you and me, if they have to." He drove through the entrance at a snail's pace, turned left, and accelerated. "By the way, Miss Cowden has just signed a paper giving away her property."

"What property?"

"Her brother's property. Instead of giving away a mere couple of hundred thousand, she is now renouncing the whole estate."

"She can't do that!"

"She thinks she can."

"Is she crazy? Who's she giving it to, for goodness' sake?"

"She hasn't the faintest idea. I have the document in my pocket, signed by her and witnessed by myself and—under protest—by Hoskins."

"Under protest is good. Hoskins knows——"

"We thought we'd like to humour her. Still, illegal as it all is, the paper itself is a rather ticklish bit of explosive to be carrying around. You know I have it. If anything should happen to me, go after it, and hand it to the lawyer, Ormville, to-morrow. He will be surprised."

"What's going to happen to you, all of a sudden?"

"Anything might, I should think, in this fog. My nerves is fiddlestrings. Hang these lamps, they don't light anything. At this rate, we shall miss at least one Celebrated Play."

CHAPTER TWELVE
Passing Bell

"'Eerie' is the word for it." Gamadge hunched his shoulders and peered obstinately at the mist, which pressed against his face like damp cotton. There were no lights but his own, and these showed nothing but a few yards of soft road, and two lines of half-visible trees. "Can this be the pleasant woodland route we followed this morning?"

"It didn't last long, you remember. We'll soon be out of it. Don't forget to turn left at the crossroads."

"I won't, if I see any crossroads." But as he spoke the air turned fresher, and he felt a hard and greasy surface under his wheels. Lights winked feebly ahead; the mist seemed thinner, out in the open. He put on speed.

After three or four minutes, Mitchell said: "Cars coming behind. I can see them making the curve as they leave the woods. One, two and three."

"Perhaps it's the rest of Callaghan's audience. I wonder if he'll wait for the gate."

Mitchell, who was leaning out to look back, said: "The last car's in a hurry. It's passed the next one; and now it's passing the first. No, they won't let him. They're speeding up. Listen to him blow his horn."

"They can all pass us, so far as I'm concerned, just so long as the idiots don't bump us."

He made way for a two-seater containing a serious-looking young man without a hat, whose spectacles gleamed wanly as he turned them on Gamadge, and two young women in peasant costume and bright headkerchiefs. The young man shouted: "…Cove?"

"Yes," shouted Gamadge.

They went on. Mitchell said: "Funny. That car is going to let the last one pass him."

"Glad of it. I don't like the sound of his horn."

"Why not? What's the matter with it?"

"Milton says the grey-fly winds a sultry horn. It must sound just like that one. Here comes Number Two."

Number Two was a family car, loaded to the fenders with father, mother, three children, and a nurse in a bonnet and uniform. Children and nurse (who was large, elderly and Irish) looked happy and expectant; father, who was driving, slowed up beside Gamadge to ask: "Going up to the Cove?"

"We're aimed that way."

"Look out for the fellow behind. He nearly had us in the ditch."

"I'll get there first, and give him the whole road."

They passed, and Gamadge had a glimpse of anguished femininity on the rear seat, controlling hysteria for the sake of its offspring.

"I guess you can't keep summer folks home, specially on a real bad night," remarked Mitchell. "They got to be out on the routes, running into one another. That last car isn't coming up; perhaps the feller's scared, now. What's a grey-fly?"

"I couldn't tell you. It must have had just such a thin, wailing note as our friend's, back there."

"Here's the turn for Tucon."

They went through Tucon from the rear, ran down the main street, swung to the entrance of the lane, and brought up with a jerk against the powerful glare of a torch.

"Hello, Trainor," said Mitchell.

"Hello, Mr. Mitchell." The policeman's rubber cape glistened as he came up to the window. "None of those people came off the place since I got here, and if they did, none of 'em came back."

"What do you mean, 'if they did'?"

"We wondered if somebody might sneak through the woods; but Jones says no."

"Jones down there now?"

"Yes, sir. Kid named Lefty Brown is our liaison officer."

"Don't you let that boy go up and down this lane any more to-night."

"No, sir. He's made his last trip."

Officer Trainor turned away, and his torch lighted up the sign that hung from the tree. Its little lantern did no more than spread a confusing gleam over the surrounding cloud of fog. At Gamadge's request, the torch remained pointing upward.

"Well, the murder's out." Gamadge laughed, as he read:

To-night at 8.45

THE OLD PIER PLAYERS

in

CATHLEEN NI HOULIHAN

THE SHADOW OF THE GLEN

THE QUEEN'S ENEMIES

"Ain't they good plays?" Mitchell also peered up at the sign.

"Oh, very. But that middle one—'The Shadow Of The Glen'—it has a corpse in it."

"My Heavens, if I'd been Callaghan, I'd have dropped it; to-night, anyway."

"Well, poor souls, they had it ready." Gamadge turned into the lane, a tunnel of quiet darkness. "Besides, it's comedy, you know."

"Comedy!"

"The corpse isn't really dead; but he might as well be, so far as anything the audience knows to the contrary, until the play's half over. But eventually he comes to life."

"And that makes it a comedy? I tell you one thing, Mr. Gamadge; perhaps it's because I ain't Irish, but I don't feel any too anxious to see it, myself. Not to-night."

"I bet anything you like that Atwood plays the corpse; it's a part he could do on his head, as I remember it."

They came out of the lane among bayberry bushes, and Gamadge drove to the end of a considerable line of cars. The Old Pier, glimmering with lights, looked a mile away. Spots of brightness marked the trailers, and paler gleams the tents. There was not a soul in sight.

"We're late, all right." Gamadge followed Mitchell down to the shore, nearly treading on his heels when he stopped to stare; and indeed what they saw was fantastic enough to give anyone pause. A group behind one of the farther trailers loomed out of the fog, picked from the embracing murk by pinpoints of light on barbaric headdresses, breastplates and spears.

"They don't seem real," said Mitchell.

"Glamour," agreed Gamadge as a figure detached itself from the group, and came forward. "Congratulations, Mrs. Atwood."

Mitchell could hardly believe his eyes; he saw before him the stately presentment of some noble Ethiopian queen, darkly implacable, jewelled from her high crown to her ankles, remote from the woman he had met that afternoon as was the Cove to-night from the Cove at midday.

"You theatre folks beat all," he said. "Won't you catch cold, Mrs. Atwood?"

"I'll have to get used to it. What did they find out about Adrienne Lake? Can't you tell me anything? We have our telephone, but Callaghan says they won't give him any satisfaction."

"They usually don't, until the analysis is all done. I guess it's safe enough to say she died of morphia poisoning."

"Morphia." Even Mrs. Atwood's voice seemed to have changed; it had a deeper tone, or so Mitchell thought; and it was echoed a moment later by the sound of a bell; a solitary note, that came to them hollowly through the fog, and died.

"Bell-buoy," said Mitchell. "Mournful, ain't it? It sounds different when there ain't any fog."

It came once more—a faint, distant boom. Mrs. Atwood spoke as it ceased.

"Atwood wanted that boy to live. He was crazy to get him up here and get hold of some of his money. That's all he did want, but he wouldn't have done anything to risk losing it. He wouldn't have hurt Amberley Cowden; he wouldn't have let anybody else hurt him. He'd have seen all the rest of us dead first."

This testament delivered, she turned back to the group, where Susie Baker's small face, also darkened and transformed, peered over Rogers' bronze shoulder. Mitchell stopped her.

"Was he working this afternoon, Mrs. Atwood?"

"No. He took time off. He was asleep in his tent."

"You know that for a fact?"

She looked at him, frowning. "Why?"

"There was some mention of his being down Ford's Beach way."

"If he was, that state policeman will know it. He was all over the place, all day."

"You wouldn't back your husband to get off this place if he wanted to, police or no police?"

"I never thought about it." She reflected, and then suddenly cast a strange, shocked look at Mitchell. "What is all this? Are you trying to make me say something that would get him in trouble?"

"I'm just trying to find out if he could have been off the place. I can't *get* him in trouble, Mrs. Atwood; if I can get answers to my questions, they may keep him out of it."

"I don't know anything about it."

She rejoined the others. Mitchell and Gamadge walked along the runway to the door of the theatre, where Gamadge insisted on purchasing two tickets.

"I regard this as my party," he said, and enquired of the young man in the béret who stood inside the entrance, "Are we very late?"

"'Cathleen' is almost over." He handed them two programmes. They went around a partition, and stood for a moment getting their bearings. The pier was in semi-darkness, the only light coming from the stage. They found their way to seats on one of the benches halfway up the aisle, and sat down.

The old fish-house turned into a theatre by the simplest and most economical process imaginable. Windows had been cut along its sides, and shutters fitted to them; lights were strung from beam to beam; and one end of the floor space—about a fifth of it—had been covered by a platform three feet high. This was divided from the auditorium by a curtain which met in the middle when closed, and could be opened as far as the operator pleased. It was widely open now, disclosing a dim interior.

"Cottage of Killala," muttered Mitchell, reading his programme by the aid of a lighted match. "Where's that?"

"Ireland. Not bad, is it? I'll have to hand it to Callaghan."

There was an ingenious arrangement of shadowy screens, a red glow to one side that might well have come from a peat fire, a candle on a rough table, and a group of four persons.

"'A Poor Old Woman, Miss Adrienne Lake,'" whispered Mitchell. "I suppose they hadn't time to change it, but it's spooky. That must be her, over to the right."

"Yes. I'd take her for Miss Lake, if I didn't know better."

"Small woman, acting old, kind of whining voice. That ain't hard to do."

"Especially as the part calls for elflocks and a head shawl. It's practically all make-up, so far; the crucial moment comes later."

"What is it all about?"

"Ssh. Allegory."

The crucial moment had arrived. Gamadge leaned forward, listening for the big line; it came, and with it the old magic, the old, authentic thrill:

"Some call me the Poor Old Woman, and there are some that call me Cathleen, the daughter of Houlihan."

Senility fell away; the voice rose, swelled, touched and held a keening note, indescribably elfin. The ancient crone changed under their eyes to something ambiguous and unearthly. She floated away, singing; her voice came back to them faintly from behind the screens.

"By Jove!" said Gamadge, aloud. "There's a new reading for you!"

Five minutes later Michael had renounced all earthly ties, and followed her; the peasants had rushed in; the singing had drifted in once more; and the curtains were beginning to tremble violently on their wires. The last two lines of the play were being spoken, and a pattering of applause had begun. It was interrupted by a loud, hollow-sounding clap or shot, which seemed to come from under their feet.

There was a moment of absolute stillness, and then Mitchell sprang up, and somebody bawled for lights. They went on, showing half the men in the audience already jamming the doorway, and the women clutching children, and one another, among the benches. Mitchell, forcibly restrained by Gamadge's grasp on his coat, shouted: "Let go. That was a shot."

"The other way, I tell you," urged Gamadge.

"What's the matter with you? There's only one door."

Actors were pouring down the aisle. Gamadge insisted: "Up there, I tell you; back of the stage."

His tone carried such absolute conviction that Mitchell was persuaded, almost against his senses, to follow him at a run up to the platform. They got on the stage, crossed it, and dodged through screens to a large dim empty space beyond. Mitchell, avoiding scenery and properties, and staring blindly about him, rounded a beam and joined Gamadge, who stood in a big double doorway, apparently contemplating infinity. There was nothing beyond but a grey void.

"What did I tell you?" panted Mitchell. "You can see from the shore that there's no ladder, and the sea comes right up to the floor timbers at high tide."

"Oh, yes; there's a ladder, flat against the side; but I don't think it goes more than halfway down. This was a landing stage, once. Got a torch?" Gamadge had turned, let himself down, and begun to disappear. When his chin was level with the door sill Mitchell had produced a torch. It showed a dim expanse of sand, to which Gamadge dropped. Mitchell tossed the flashlight gently down to him, and followed.

They went into the velvety blackness under the pier, with the torch lighting up a foot or two of brown sand ahead of them, or shining to this side and that on a forest of piles; a dead forest, with angular branches that dripped wetly, and a murky sky above it. When Gamadge swung the light in a low half circle they could see the debris left by the last tide; kelp, clam shells, pebbles, bits of iridescent bottle glass, a stranded jellyfish. Mitchell slipped on one of these, staggered, and bumped against a slippery pile.

"You think somebody went out by that back door?" he asked.

"I know he did. Never thought of it until I grabbed you. There was water all around the place to-day, and I didn't realise that it would be dry land to-night before the tide came."

"How do you know he did?"

"Because he didn't come down the aisle."

"Who was it?"

"Atwood, of course. Didn't you see him on the stage?"

"There was half a dozen men on the stage. I didn't notice him. You sure he was there?"

"Of course I am."

"Funny I didn't recognise him."

"I shouldn't have, if I hadn't been watching for him."

Lights appeared ahead of them, like shrouded fireflies; and suddenly a torch swung upward and blinded them.

"Oh, hello, Mr. Mitchell," said a voice, and the light dropped.

"Hello, Cal. Find anything?"

The torch came to rest on what looked like a bundle of old clothes, huddled on the sand. "I don't know what it's all about," complained the state policeman. "I was at the trailer, and I heard the shot." He shifted the light, and Gamadge saw a hand, with a pistol lying near it. "Who is this woman? Did she kill herself?"

"Dead, is she?" Mitchell bent and lifted the slight, bony wrist.

"Yes. The bullet hole's under her hair, right between the eyes."

"Well, you ride up, fast as you can, and tell Trainor not to pass anybody out unless he positively knows 'em for summer folks that came through to the show; and he's to take their names and addresses before they go home. Tell him not to pass anybody at all, riding alone. The line here is fixed; get through to Cogswell."

The officer faded into mist, and a crowd of staring faces pressed up about the body on the sand. Some of them were painted, some surmounted by outlandish headdresses. Mrs. Atwood's barbaric crown moved into the circle, and her anklets jingled as she slipped on a great strand of kelp. Callaghan was beside her.

"Holy angels," he said, in a flat voice. He stood looking down at the dead face, glistening with grease paint, that seemed to gaze back at him from sunken eyes half-hidden under a fringe of straggling grey hair.

"Keep back, you folks." Mitchell jabbed vaguely towards the circle with his torch. "Who is this woman, Callaghan?"

Callaghan did not seem to hear the question. "Holy angels," he repeated, and then, turning to Mrs. Atwood, admonished her gently: "Go away, now, Floss; this is no place for you."

"I'm all right." She raised her eyes from the staring eyes to meet Gamadge's. "He was right about you, wasn't he?" she said.

CHAPTER THIRTEEN
Death of an Understudy

Mitchell, confused and impatient, repeated sharply: "Why can't some of you say who it is?"

Gamadge glanced at him as if in surprise. "It's Atwood."

"Atwood!"

"Yes. He gave a fine performance, Mrs. Atwood. It was a new reading of the part, though, wasn't it? Did he get it from Adrienne Lake?"

Far from resenting this unemotional question, Mrs. Atwood seemed to welcome the chance thus given to discuss her husband impersonally. "It was his," she said. "He was always trying to get her to do it that way."

Mitchell, after a stupefied look at Gamadge, knelt down on one knee, removed the scarlet head shawl, and stripped off the grey wig. Atwood's reptilian head sprang into view, unmistakable in spite of a mask of paint and wrinkles. He looked at the hands, and at the pistol. Both were greasy with paint.

"He wanted me to come up and see him in this part," he reflected, aloud. "Why?"

"Because he knew you'd find out that he'd been rehearsing it for hours yesterday. That right, Callaghan?"

"He was at it all evening, and up to ten o'clock. He volunteered when she gave up, about six; and he gave me a sample of what he could do. I ditched her regular understudy, and let him do it. She went out to the pier with him, and started him off; the rest of us left them at it. We were dead-beat—we've pretty well rebuilt this place, since the beginning of the week, you know."

"And Miss Lake turned in herself, leaving him at work?"

"Yes. I went out and gave him a look-in at about eight—that's when the telephone message came for him from Tucon. We were going to make a stunt of it, and feature him after he'd fooled a couple of audiences. It ought to have gone big."

Gamadge said: "Somebody must have done that last singing for him, behind the scenes."

"I did." A tall girl in a plaid shawl pushed forward. "He came behind, and he said: 'Can you give them the last of it, Mab? I've got to go and change.' He was in the Synge play with me, the next one."

"So he went down the ladder?"

"Yes. I didn't know where he'd got to, till I looked. I never knew there was a ladder there at all."

"This is Miss Mabel Burke," said Callaghan, "one of our most talented ladies. She could have played Cathleen, but her part in 'The Shadow' is a tough one, enough for one evening. Sure, you gave them time to kill him and get away with it, Mab. It's a nice favour you did him."

For the moment, Mitchell ignored this. "Isn't his tent right beside the shore? It wouldn't be but a few yards from the end of the pier; yet he's way under it." He gently turned the body on its side. "I don't see any torch."

"Then they got him under, or carried him under."

"This is supposed to be a suicide, Callaghan." Mitchell rose, and slapped at the damp sand on his trouser leg.

"If it is, then I'm a Chinaman. Did you ever see him in better spirits, Floss?"

Mrs. Atwood was standing, half-turned from the body, her arms folded. She answered: "He wouldn't kill himself, no matter what happened."

"Perhaps you'll tell us who shot him, then," said Mitchell, politely.

"It's a mystery to me," answered Callaghan. "Nobody here would think of it. What do you say, Floss?"

"Nobody," she replied.

Gamadge had for some time been conscious that his heels were sinking into the sand. He now said, "You'll have to move him, Mitchell; the tide's coming in."

"I've moved him already, you'll notice. Here, you two fellows, Rogers, and the boy in the leopard skins, there; you go get some kind of a stretcher. Callaghan, I want you to round up all your people, and send the ticket-seller over to Jones, the trooper, so he can check up on the audience. If we can sort out the ones that were on the pier when it happened, we can send them home. Off with you, now, you folks." He added: "Why don't some of you women take Mrs. Atwood up there and give her a rug to put on her, and a drink of something hot? She's shivering with a chill, and no wonder."

Callaghan took her by the arm, and they went off together, with the crowd. A wet shimmer had appeared on the floor of the Cove, and Gamadge felt a cool breath of air against his cheek.

"The mist is thinning," he said.

"It'll be gone with the tide." Mitchell picked up the pistol, slipped the safety catch, and wrapped it in his handkerchief. He stowed it in his pocket, remarking: "Cogswell will think there's something mighty queer about this place, even if this does turn out to be suicide. It might be. We don't know, yet, what he had on his mind."

Gamadge said: "I think I know one thing that was on it, all right. That alibi of his is no good."

"No good! Why, it's the only thing we *are* sure of, so far as it goes, which ain't far enough, by a jugful. You think these people are all lying?"

"No. I think he fooled them. I don't believe he rehearsed that part last night one minute after eight o'clock, when Callaghan saw him, and the Brown boy heard him. I think Miss Adrienne Lake played her own part. Remember the mist, and remember his make-up; do you suppose they could have been told apart?"

"But she was sick. Why would she do such a thing?"

"Well, you found fifty dollars on her, Mitchell; and they say she had no money at all."

"Atwood's supposed to have paid her to rehearse her own part, last night? So he could get off the place?"

"Yes; and no living person can break his alibi. Miss Lake is dead."

Mitchell looked down at the body at their feet, over the head of which he had thrown the red shawl. Then he said: "Fixed that, too, did he?"

"I'm inclined to think so. How, we don't yet know; but we may possibly find out. Mr. Arthur Atwood," said Gamadge, sombrely, "was a clever fellow; but like all clever fellows, he thought nobody else was as intelligent as he was. I wonder how he felt, when he dropped down from that ladder, and saw the pistol coming up through the mist, two inches from his face? He'd back right under the pier, and he'd keep going until he was shot. You were well-advised not to waste time looking for the person that pulled the trigger, Mitchell."

"I knew we couldn't find anybody in that fog."

"Not with such a head start as that."

"Perhaps Trainor…"

"Perhaps."

The two young men in their leopard skins and bronze armour arrived, with a blanket stretched across their spears. Atwood's body was lifted on it, and the cortège moved slowly out into the open. Somebody had backed a car down to the shore; its headlamps illuminated the scene in a sudden bath of white light. Officer Jones roared across the clearing on his motorcycle; one or two cars were driving off; and a huddled group of summer visitors waited beside their cars. The actors sat or stood among the trailers, rugs cast about their shoulders, coffee cups passing from hand to hand.

Atwood's body was placed in Adrienne Lake's caravan, and then Mitchell addressed the Old Pier Players:

"Now, folks; stands to reason that Atwood wouldn't go down there under that pier and shoot himself for no reason at all. Suppose he got some bad news? Any messages come down from Tucon?"

"Not a one. We have our telephone, now," said Callaghan.

"Did he get a call on the telephone?"

"Not this evening. So far as I know, not all day."

"Well, how about a visitor? I want to know if any of you saw anybody down here to-night that didn't belong on the place. Any stranger wandering around, looking like a member of the audience, perhaps, but keeping off the pier. Anybody at all."

Susie Baker spoke tremulously from the enveloping folds of her blanket: "Only the telephone man."

"What telephone man?"

"He was back of Miss Lake's trailer, working on the pole, or something."

"Where was Jones, the state policeman?"

"He'd gone across to the tents to get some coffee."

"I thought the telephone people left."

"There was just this one man. He was only back there a minute, and then he went down the bank."

"Any of the rest of you see him?"

One other girl had noticed him, but neither she nor Susie could describe him; he had been a shadow among shadows, a phantom of the mist. They had thought him a telephone man because telephone men had been working there for days, and because he wore a peaked cap.

"He waited for Atwood down on the bank, below his tent," said Gamadge, when they had moved out of ear-shot. "Atwood must have come down the ladder almost on top of him. Pleasant surprise all round."

"If Trainor's let him through——"

"Why shouldn't Trainor have let him through? I'll go up and have a word with him. Don't look so desperate, Mitchell; all is not lost. That telephone man was one of the few living persons that expected to find Atwood under a head shawl. There's Mrs. Atwood—I want to speak to her."

Mrs. Atwood sat by herself on the stump she seemed to prefer as a resting place, drinking coffee from a mug. Her glittering crown had been removed, and she had thrown a loose coat over her shoulders. Gamadge said: "Now, that's sensible. I hope there's a stick in that."

"There is; brandy."

"Look here, Mrs. Atwood; I do wish you could see your way to helping us out a little. Poor Susie Baker's a material witness; she may be in for all sorts of inconvenience and bother if the police can't find out where that morphia came from. No dentist gives anybody morphia for an abscessed tooth; it's ridiculous."

Mrs. Atwood said nothing.

"Your husband's dead," continued Gamadge. "It's a question now of considering the living—and the innocent Susie Baker saw him coming home to the Cove at three o'clock last night."

"What!"

"And we have reason to think that he paid Miss Lake to go out there on the pier from eight to ten, and impersonate herself."

Mrs. Atwood's mouth fell open.

"Couldn't it have been worked? Just think back, and see whether it couldn't."

Mrs. Atwood looked about her as if she hardly knew where she was. At last she said, "Perhaps it could. I don't know anything about it."

"You wouldn't. The point is, there really isn't any use fighting to preserve Atwood's reputation. That's hopeless. But one word from you might send that little Baker girl home to her family without any trouble or delay."

Mrs. Atwood cogitated, and seemed suddenly to make up her mind. "Adrienne Lake wasn't taking morphia," she said harshly. "The dentist gave her something to rub on her tooth; that's all."

"She hadn't anything at all to help her sleep?"

"She had aspirin."

"Aspirin!" Mitchell repeated it blankly.

"That's all she ever took."

"You seemed surprised when we told you it was morphia, ma'am; very much surprised."

"I was."

"Your husband didn't possess any, so far as you know?" She gave him a questioning look. After a moment she said: "He used to have some. He never could stand pain—not a twinge. No aspirin for him!"

"I'm obliged to you. Just one question more—routine. You were with some of the others while this shooting was going on?"

"Yes. I didn't kill Arthur," she said with a stiff smile. Gamadge left them. On his way to his car he stopped in front of Callaghan, who stood alone in the middle of the clearing, hands on hips and legs straddled. He was watching his public depart. His lower lip jutted out, and he looked defeated, yet indomitable.

"I'm awfully sorry about all this," said Gamadge. "It's the rottenest kind of luck. I wouldn't take it too hard, though; this business may actually draw people, instead of putting them off."

"I hope you're right."

"And I don't think you're going to have any police trouble, to speak of."

"I'll have trouble finding another Atwood. He was only half human, sorry as I am to say so; but he was clever, and I needed him. Tell me, now; did you ever see anything cleverer than that show he put on to-night?"

"It was remarkable. Famous for female impersonations, wasn't he?"

"He was, and his father before him."

"I gathered that he was going to play Cathleen from what was said up here this afternoon; and somebody told me about the female impersonating, which clinched it for me."

"He told me you had an evil eye."

"Oh, that was only because I intimated that the gods were about to destroy him. He didn't like that."

"And how did you know they were about to destroy him?"

"He finally gave me the tip himself. Well, good luck to you. I'm staying at the Ocean House, Ford's Beach; let me know if I can do anything for Mrs. Atwood."

"She'll stay on here with me, and so will the others—if I can feed them."

"You'll feed them, don't worry. Only for Heaven's sake drop that play with the corpse in it! Put a funny one in the bill. Don't the Irish ever write funny plays?"

"They're famous for it."

"Then dig some up, that's my advice to you."

He got into his car, and drove away from the desolate reaches of Seal Cove. At the other end of the lane Officer Trainor was at the car window before Gamadge saw him, and stopped.

"What is all this?" he asked, from the running board. "Cal Jones said he didn't know anything, and he wouldn't wait a second. I can't ask the folks in the cars!"

"No; very humiliating. One of the actors was shot, and it probably wasn't suicide. Did you pass any sort of mechanic into the lane to-night?"

"Only the telephone feller."

"Late on the job, wasn't he?"

"He came back for some gear they left. He was the next in after you, and he came back five minutes before Cal Jones got here with the news."

"He's home by now. Did you notice his car?"

"I didn't take the number of it; why should I? It was an old green Dodge sedan."

"The grey-fly. Did you get a look at the fellow?"

"Half his face under the cap, with a streak of grease across it."

"This seems to be a costume piece. You wouldn't know him again, I gather?"

"Say, what is all this, anyway?" Trainor had one leg over his machine. "I can phone in an alarm."

"Useless. You couldn't say whether this lineman was young or old, man, woman, or boy. Now, could you?"

"I'd have said he was a feller about my age."

"Say so now?"

"You've got me all mixed up."

"Did he speak to you?"

"Word or two. He talked slow and husky; had a cough."

"You know what I'd do if I were you, Trainor? I'd take a chance and quit this job. When you tell Mitchell what you've just told me, he'll know your work is over, up here. He can use you at the Cove."

"I don't know."

"He'll want to hear about this telephone man. Tell him to drop in at the Ocean House later—no matter how late. I'll have that report he wanted, or some of it."

The family car which had passed Gamadge on the road earlier in the evening drove up, bulging with clamorous children.

"Name, sir, please." Trainor automatically got out his notebook.

"Newberry. Who was it got shot, officer?"

"One of the actors. Where are you staying?"

"The Gunket, the Gunket, the Gunket," shouted a child, and another implored: "Oh, Daddy, don't let's go home yet. Let's wait and find out who killed him."

The back seat spoke, in no uncertain terms: "We're going back to Ogunquit just as fast as we can get there."

"And I didn't think much of the play," complained the far from Neo-Celt beside her, clutching a child as the car began to move. "When I saw 'The Shaughraun'——"

Gamadge started his coupé, and prepared to follow. "Don't forget to ask Mitchell to see me at the Ocean House, no matter how late," he said.

He took the back road. There was no longer much fog, and on this second trip he made better time than he had made that afternoon. He reached the Ocean House at ten minutes past ten.

CHAPTER FOURTEEN
The Door Is Open

The hotel was blazing with lights from tower to basement. Several cars were parked in front, and Gamadge drove on down to the garage, the rumble of the freight elevator in his ears. Officer Loomis was sitting in converse with Kimball, the night man, beside a long, low, shining bulk that Gamadge recognised as the Cowden touring car.

"Nobody's been near it," said Loomis. "Young feller came in, asked for the road maps. I got them out and give them to him. He asked what I was doin' there, and I said, mindin' my own business."

"That was in the nature of a hint, wasn't it?"

"I didn't like the drawly way he talked. Had his head up, and looked down the sides of his nose."

Gamadge laughed at this graphic description of Fred Barclay's technique when surprised or annoyed, and walked back to the Ocean House. He passed slowly along the row of cars, paused before an old green Dodge sedan, and leaning in through a window, gently pressed the horn. It emitted a thin, angry wail, very like a mosquito's. He went on into the hotel.

The lobby was a scene of moderate festivity. The log fire blazed merrily; four or five bridge tables were going; and several incoming guests were signing up at the desk. Gamadge stopped beside a table where Doctor Baines, Mrs. Baines, Mr. Macpherson and an elderly lady in a white shawl were finishing a rubber. He watched for a moment and then passed on to the stairs. Peabody and Waldo were hurrying about with bottles of ginger ale and clean ash trays, and Wilks, behind the counter, was doing a lively trade in chocolate bars and cigarettes. They all noticed him, and he nodded to each.

He climbed the stairs, and went down the corridor toward Number 22. Luggage was now piled in front of doors; a truck stood just within the fire escape, and Hoskins, from his rocking chair within the room, contemplated it gravely.

"All serene?" inquired Gamadge.

"Is now. We've had some baggage haulin'."

"So I see. How is the Cowden party?"

"Not a peep out of 'em. The Barclays came about 8.15."

"Still here?"

"Yes. The Colonel's in there with Mrs. Cowden; Waldo got him some ginger ale, 'bout an hour ago. Mrs. Barclay and the young feller have been playin' Russian bank in Room 17. It's been open, since they printed it."

"I saw a light going in there."

"Mr. Sanderson went to bed. He must be asleep by now—his light's off."

"And nobody's been in or out by the fire escape, I suppose?"

"Nobody but the porters."

"I see. Well, Hoskins, I'm sorry to have to tell you that you've been hoist by your own petard."

Hoskins looked bewildered.

"They have fooled you to the top of your bent. I suppose that new porter was wearing the uniform they took away from this room while you were asleep. And I bet he was carrying something big on his shoulder, both times you saw him. I mean, when he left here soon after I did, and came back a little while ago."

"What you talking about?"

"You didn't see his face, now did you?"

"I wouldn't say I did. I wasn't noticin'."

"You might find out whether there *is* another porter."

Gamadge left him wildly calling the office, and started back down the corridor. He paused in front of Room 19, the door of which was rattling; too bad, he thought; it might wake her. He felt in his pocket for a bit of paper or a card to use as a wedge, and suddenly realised that the door was not latched.

The almost imperceptible crack widened, closed, and widened again. Casting a glance up at the dark transom, he gently pushed the door open, and listened. The room was black, and at first he heard nothing; then, after a long interval, came a long, rasping breath. He fumbled for the switch, could not find it, and crossed the room in the direction of the bed table. He found the lamp, and jerked the light on.

The girl's face was dusky against the pillow, and it seemed ages before the harsh breath came again. He glanced swiftly at a small bottle and a medicine glass on the nightstand, and then tore Alma Cowden out of the bed, blankets and all. As he dashed out of the doorway, he had a dim impression of Hoskins standing in front of Number 22, with his mouth open; but he was not at the moment concerned with Hoskins. He ran down the corridor to the last room on the right, and assaulted the lower panel with his toe.

Doctor and Mrs. Baines came up behind him. Gamadge gasped: "Emergency," waited while the doctor silently opened the door and put on the light, and then deposited Miss Cowden and her blankets on one of the twin beds. "I don't know what she's taken," he said. "I'm going back for the bottle."

Hoskins materialised in the doorway, peering over Mrs. Baines' broad shoulder. "I'll get it," he said, and disappeared.

The doctor's bulk concealed the patient, as he bent over her. Presently he straightened and addressed his wife, who stood transfixed, her flowered silk skirts billowing about her in the draught from the hall:

"Come in and close the door, Mollie. Have we mustard? You didn't leave it at home just this once? Good. I want some mustard and warm water, and then you can start making coffee."

Mrs. Baines shut the door behind her, and went into the bathroom. Baines turned to Gamadge. "Send down for the boy Waldo," he ordered, and again bent over the figure on the bed.

Gamadge picked up the telephone and got the office. When he looked around, Hoskins was back in the room, offering the bottle and the glass to Baines.

"What's the matter with her?" Events had been too much for Hoskins; he looked terrified, as if feeling that he had been subjected to the machinations of some djinn.

"Juice of the poppy, in some form. What's this stuff?" He read from a handwritten label: "'Orange-flower Water.' Where'd you find this?"

"On the table by her bed. And the glass, too."

Baines squinted at the label again, removed the cork, and sniffed at the contents with an expression of extreme abhorrence.

"It appears to be a sickly syrup, unknown to the pharmacopœia. If it is some of Lulu Barclay's witches' brew, I'll make an example of her."

"Mis' Barclay's been tryin' to give her medicine, all day," chattered Hoskins.

"She would. How did you come to find the girl like this, Gamadge?"

"I knew she was keeping her door locked, saw that it was open, and investigated."

"Lucky for her you did. Stuff ready, Mollie? Into the hall with you two, then. I'll be with you."

Waldo rushed up, as they waited. Presently Baines came out, closing the door after him, and Gamadge asked: "Could you use a nurse, sir?"

"I could use three."

"Miss Macpherson ought to be here by this time."

"Excellent idea. You—what's your name?—Hoskins. Go and find Miss Macpherson. Quiet, now; no publicity."

Hoskins again vanished. Baines had produced a fountain pen and tablets from some inner vastness of his coat, and wrote furiously. He then looked at Waldo, and asked: "Is your father at home, this evening?"

"Yes, sir. I think he is."

"Has he a partner?"

"Yes, sir."

"Get one or the other of them on the telephone; I want these things as soon as possible, and they'll have to be brought by somebody that won't talk about it. Can you read this writing?"

Waldo gazed at the sheet of paper which had been thrust under his nose, and said he could.

"Got a nickel? I want you to telephone from the booth."

"Yes, Doctor."

"Ask your father to call up the hospital he's connected with—Bailtown, is it?"

"Yes."

"They're to send an ambulance. And if he can think of anything else to send besides the tube, the hypodermic, the atropine, and the permanganate of potash, I'll be obliged for it. He'll know the urgency of the case without your having to tell him. Off with you."

Waldo sped away. Mrs. Baines, putting her head through the door, said:

"Where's Eleanor Cowden? Have you told her?"

"I had no time, Mrs. Baines," explained Gamadge.

"You must go and tell her now."

Miss Macpherson, shepherded by Hoskins, came down the hall. She was a brawny, red-haired young woman, whose rocklike professional calm had not been affected by the facts that her hair was coming down, both her shoe-laces were untied, and her jumper sticking halfway down her broad torso. She tugged at it as she advanced.

"This is good of you, Miss Macpherson," said Baines. "Emergency case. You stay around, Gamadge. When and if we get her on her feet, she'll have to be walked; and I can't do it. I'm too old, and I'm too fat."

"Get Mrs. Cowden," repeated Mrs. Baines, and Gamadge was left with Hoskins outside the door.

Hoskins looked utterly chopfallen. "Was it my fault?" he asked, anxiously.

"No, of course not. I should never have seen that the door was open myself, if I hadn't started to wedge it. I suppose whoever closed it last didn't spend that extra half second required to make sure that it was properly latched. These old locks are all loose."

"And you could unlock 'em with a penknife or a nail file. I guess I must have turned my back, Mr. Gamadge. I'm awfully sorry. She looked pretty bad. Can they save her?"

"Don't ask me, I don't know. Baines said 'if,' and that's bad. Funny we didn't bring the place around our ears."

"Well, you have rubber soles, and my sneakers don't make any noise at all."

"You stick around, will you? I have to break it to Mrs. Cowden, and we may need another doctor. Even she can't be expected to go on for ever without crashing."

He knocked on the door of Room 21. The low-voiced conversation that he could hear through the transom ceased, and Mrs. Cowden's voice asked him to come in. She and the Colonel sat at her table, busy with lists and telegraph forms.

"Back already?" She looked up at him in surprise.

"Yes. I'm very sorry, Mrs. Cowden, but Doctor Baines wants me to tell you that Miss Cowden has taken some medicine, and it hasn't agreed with her."

"Taken what?" She sat back, her face stiffening.

"Some medicine or other. She's in their room. He and Mrs. Baines are working on her, and they got hold of a nurse."

She got up slowly, gripping the edge of the table. The Colonel rose also, his eyes protruding. "Now, Eleanor. Now, Eleanor," he began, as she swayed a little.

"I'm all right. In the Baineses' room, you say?"

"Just sit down a minute, Mrs. Cowden." Gamadge eased her into her chair. "They're doing everything, and they've sent for another doctor, and an ambulance."

"Medicine? What medicine? I don't understand. She only had what Bertie Baines gave her."

"We don't know where it came from. The bottle says 'Orange-flower Water.'"

She turned her chalky face and looked at the Colonel. "Now, Eleanor," he stammered.

"But the symptoms seem to point to morphia, in some form," Gamadge went on.

Mrs. Cowden repeated: "Morphia?" She got to her feet, and walked stiffly out of the room, like a woman in a trance. Gamadge watched her until she was safely through the Baineses' doorway, and then betook himself to Room 22. Here, after an interval, the Barclay family sought him; Mrs. Barclay pale and apparently very angry, the Colonel shaken, their son impassive, except for the clenching and unclenching of his hands.

"What's all this, Gamadge?" he asked, keeping his voice well under control.

"Miss Cowden seems to have had another accident." Gamadge offered Mrs. Barclay a chair, but she ignored it.

"Morphia!" she exclaimed, scornfully. "Morphia in Aunt Julia's Orange-flower Water! The most harmless tonic! We all take it."

"You'd much better tell us exactly what's in the stuff, Lulu." The Colonel's voice trembled. "It may be a matter of life and death."

"I have a recipe somewhere; we've been taking it for years, Mr. Gamadge."

"You're right, we have," said Lieutenant Barclay, "and it didn't do worse than turn our stomachs. Sure you didn't put something else in it, this time? Accidents will happen, even to you druggists."

"To-night I added a few of those little pills you had when you broke your arm, Fred. They gave you many a good night's rest."

Fred Barclay and his father exchanged a long, blank look. "Codeine?" gasped the Colonel. "Lulu, are out of your senses?"

"If they hurt Alma, she has an idiosyncrasy. Codeine is perfectly harmless."

"How much did you put in?" asked her son, with elaborate patience.

"Just what was left in the phial. It couldn't have amounted to more than a grain or so."

"A grain or so. Very reassuring. When did you give her the dose?"

"When we first came; she'd just had her dinner. I slipped in from Eleanor's room, to say good night."

"Waited while she drank it, did you?"

"The child was so sweet about it; she took it all."

"Poor old Alma. How much codeine does it take to kill people, Gamadge? Have you any idea?"

"A good deal, I imagine. It wasn't by any chance plain morphia, was it, Mrs. Barclay?"

"No, it was not!"

"Did the phial it came out of have a label on it?"

"It only said: 'Quarter-grain tablets.'"

"Oh, yes; a prescription."

Young Barclay got a flask out of his pocket. "Well, Mum," he said, "if Alma pulls through, I don't think they can do a thing to you. If she doesn't, Aunt Eleanor will have your life, anyway, so you needn't worry about what the verdict will be. We'd better have a drink on it."

"That's enough, my boy." The Colonel's face was mottled, and he had sunk into the chair his wife had refused. His son brought him neat whisky in the top of the flask, and stood over him while he drank it. He then poured some more for his mother, who downed it as if, in spite of her injured attitude, she needed it badly. "Baines will get her out of it," said the Colonel, recovering a little.

"You saw her, Gamadge; what did you think of her?" Young Barclay offered Gamadge a drink, and when it was refused, swallowed it himself.

"I must confess I thought she was pretty far gone, but I have no experience in morphia poisoning," replied Gamadge, who felt unable, at the moment, to mince words.

Colonel Barclay got up and trotted out of the room and down the hall. He returned with Doctor Baines, who addressed Mrs. Barclay briskly:

"Well, Lulu; I hear that you've been dosing little Alma Cowden."

"It couldn't possibly have hurt her, Bertie; she must have taken something else."

"How is she?" Fred Barclay, who was standing beside one of the windows, asked the question without turning his head.

"Can't tell yet. It was touch and go when this young man brought her in. Have you any more of that—er—that tonic of yours, Lulu?"

"I have a supply of it, yes."

"Exactly what you gave Alma?"

"Of course."

"Are you sure those tablets you added to the stuff were codeine?"

Mrs. Barclay replied uneasily, "Of course they were."

"Where's the doctor that gave you the prescription?"

"He's in Mitchy Pitchy."

"Where?"

"Some place in Peru, I think he said."

"Oh. Well, if he's in Machu Picchu, we won't be able to get hold of him to-night, anyway. Who's your druggist?"

"Thorwald, on Madison Avenue. We've dealt with him since——"

"So have I. Have *you* been taking codeine until you can tolerate any amount of that stuff?"

"If you are insinuating, Bertie Baines, that I am a drug addict——"

"Well, Lulu, I don't know what else you can call yourself. Now listen to me carefully, because this is serious. *Was* it codeine in that bottle? It takes a powerful lot of codeine to hurt anybody."

"It was little bits of tablets, quarter grain, and Freddy had one every four hours, and he wasn't to have more than four. And there were just a few left, and I pounded them up and put them in the little bottle. And I shook it up, and Alma couldn't have got anywhere nearly as much as Fred did."

"But were they codeine, Lulu? Look here. When the ambulance comes, I'm sending specimens back with it for analysis. I'll eat my hat if that girl in there hasn't absorbed more than two grains of morphia. What I'm getting at is this: Suppose you put a little morphia in the bottle Alma took the dose out of to-night; and I'll be hanged, by the way, if I know how you persuaded her to swallow it."

"I just stood there and argued with her, and told her how much good it did Freddy, and what a nice sleep he had after it, and she said, very rudely, poor child, that she saw she wouldn't get any sleep at all if I didn't go; and she took the glass and drank it right down."

"You ought to be a trained nurse. The thing is, Lulu, that they're going to find a lot of that morphia when they make the analysis. If somebody tampered with your family tonic after you doctored it yourself——"

Young Barclay swung around, and advanced a step. The tone in which he spoke can only be described as a snarl: "What are you talking about?"

"Listen, and you'll find out, my lad; and don't try to intimidate me, if you know what's good for you. Your mother is in serious trouble. If Alma dies, and there's an inquest, and your mother talks on the witness stand as she is talking to me, I won't answer for the consequences. I'm trying to find out how Alma got this morphia into her, and I haven't much time to do it in. I suggest that more may have been added to the tonic, or that Alma may have taken other tablets, earlier or later."

Colonel Barclay said huskily: "Tell him what you know, Lulu."

Mrs. Barclay suddenly burst into a flood of tears.

"They were morphia tablets," she sobbed. "Little bits of ones."

"And how many did you put in?"

"Four."

"One grain. Alma got more of the stuff somehow. Well, you and Barclay had better toddle off home, and I'm sending that little deputy Hoskins along with you, to collect the bottle. I'll check up with Thorwald and find out how many tablets were in the morphia prescription, and you'll swear Fred had four of them, and Alma had four."

"That's all there were."

"Very likely. I'll have the Orange-flower Water—bah! I'll have it analysed, too. You stay here, Fred; I shall need you."

Mrs. Barclay had somewhat recovered her dignity. "Let the man go with the Colonel," she said. "I have no intention of leaving Eleanor while that child is in danger."

"I regret to say that Eleanor has lost her head, for the moment. She is informing all comers that you meant to murder her niece, Lulu, so that Fred would get half of Amberley's money. What do you think of that?"

Mrs. Barclay stared at him, her mouth open. Fred Barclay, after a moment or two of immobility, swung back to the window. He said, over his shoulder: "Hard as nails; I always knew it. And a good deal more likely to commit murder for money than any of the Barclays are, I should say."

Baines replied equably: "She is not cerebrating at the moment; and she is not a possible suspect where her niece by marriage is concerned, young fellow. If Alma should die of this, which the gods forbid, the boy's money—her money—goes to her natural heirs, you know."

"Thanks for reminding me of it." Fred Barclay's voice was toneless.

"Don't forget it. Well, off you go, then, Barclay; I think that's all for to-night; unless," and he regarded Mrs. Barclay thoughtfully, "you'd like to come clean, Lulu, as my favourite novelists would express it, and tell me why Alma Cowden took your medicine. Young Gamadge here says he warned her off it absolutely."

Fred Barclay scowled. "Gamadge——" he began, angrily.

"He has his useful moments. Well, Lulu?"

Mrs. Barclay looked terrified, drew a long breath, and said: "Bertie, you'll never forgive me. I told her you had ordered it."

To her amazement, Baines gave a chuckling laugh. "Good for you, Lulu! I swear I never should have thought you'd come out with it. I won't tell Eleanor Cowden."

The Colonel said, choking: "I'm amazed that you should listen to her criminal nonsense, Baines. There's no excuse for it."

"I'm cooped up in the room with her, and I have to listen. But you don't; not now. Now, just to oblige me, take yourselves off."

Mrs. Barclay suddenly burst into a flood of tears, but the Colonel had pulled himself together.

"Wisest thing to do," he said. "No wonder Eleanor is half out of her head. She'll forget all about this. Come along, Lulu."

Hoskins, looking solemn and somewhat frightened, appeared in the doorway, and all three of them went down the hall, Mrs. Barclay in the middle. Baines, his lower lip pushed out, watched them go; then he said cheerfully:

"Now, then; you get Sanderson out of bed, Gamadge, and wait till I call you. I'll put you all in quarter-hour shifts; Miss Macpherson says she'll help, and we'll need her. It's about as hard a job as there is. Take your coat off."

Forty-five minutes later, when the ambulance arrived, Gamadge was supine on the couch in the Baineses' sitting room, with Miss Macpherson, also exhausted, in an armchair beside him; Mrs. Baines was administering coffee to them both; Mrs. Cowden lay flat on one of the beds in Room 1, while Doctor Baines, coat and collar long discarded, fanned her with a newspaper; and Fred Barclay and Sanderson dragged the all but inanimate form of Alma Cowden back and forth by way of the bathroom, perspiration streaming down their faces.

"Don't be a fool now," reiterated the doctor. "She's coming along nicely. She's better. Can't you see she's walking? Sit up now, like a good girl, and take some black coffee."

But Mrs. Cowden remained motionless; she did not even rise to see her niece put on the stretcher and carried away.

The three young men came out into the corridor. Young Barclay went on downstairs without a word to the others, but Sanderson detained Gamadge.

"My God," he said, "this is unbelievable. I wish I knew what Baines really thought about her chances. Mrs. Cowden says—is it true that fool of a Barclay woman put morphia in Alma's medicine?"

"Yes."

"The old harpy ought to be in jail." He looked very wild, his fair hair hanging over his eyes and his colour chalky. "Thank Heaven you noticed the door. I thought she was keeping it locked—wasn't she?"

"Alma? Yes. She was supposed to be keeping it locked."

"But if—didn't Mrs. Barclay go through from Mrs. Cowden's room?"

"Yes."

"Then who unlocked the door?"

"I have no evidence."

"Atwood must have been up at the Cove."

"Yes, he was. He still is. Now, do let me go up and turn in. I'm ready to drop, and so must you be."

He went upstairs, leaving Sanderson distraught and bewildered in the corridor, and entered his room. He had got out of his clothes and into his pyjamas when his telephone rang.

"That you, Mitchell?" he asked. "Come right up. Yes, big doings; too big—I'm signing off. You'll have to take over now. Oh—I found the green Dodge sedan. Come up and I'll tell you all about it."

CHAPTER FIFTEEN
Mr. Ormville Is Aghast

When Mr. Ormville, the lawyer, arrived early next morning, he seemed more amused than annoyed to find a deputy sheriff asleep in his room. He was a tall, slim, distinguished old gentleman, beautifully turned out in dark-grey flannels, and he wore a folding pair of tortoise-shell eyeglasses on a black ribbon. Sam was a little afraid of him; he was, besides, outraged by Hoskins' presence in Room 22.

"You know you hadn't any business stayin' here all night," he said. "We loaned you the room yesterday just to accommodate the Cowdens. What's the idea?"

"Never mind." Mr. Ormville tipped Sam, whose long vigil, just coming to an end, had left him looking rather wan, and watched him leave with a benignant smile.

"I'm awful sorry." Hoskins collected his collar and coat, and hastily pushed his feet into his shoes. "I know I should have went last night, but I didn't realise this room was engaged for you, and I was up till all hours workin' on the case."

"Very sensible of you to stay on here... What case?"

Hoskins stared. "Why, this—this case we was all workin' on. I thought you was workin' on it, too. I thought you was their lawyer."

"I am their lawyer, and I came to be of service to them; I have not been informed that there was a 'case.'"

This detachment, coming after the alarms of the past twenty-four hours, staggered Hoskins. He was about to reply, but Mr. Ormville went blandly on: "I want a wash and a shave, and then I shall go down and get some coffee. Will you join me in the dining-room?"

Hoskins said he would. Still rather embarrassed and bemused, he looked about the room, and asked: "Would you like I should fix things up for you? The chambermaids don't come on till eight."

"No, thank you very much. This will do very well."

Hoskins seized his partly used towel from the bathroom and fled down the hall to the public lavatory. He washed, brushed his hair with his fingers, and awaited Mr. Ormville at the foot of the stairs. That gentleman, when he arrived, looked to the eye of Hoskins no more immaculate than he had before, if perhaps slightly refreshed. They went into the dining-room, and Mr. Ormville ordered for both. When the waitress had gone, Hoskins said:

"I took the liberty of callin' up the sheriff and tellin' him you was here."

"Very thoughtful of you. Did you arrange an appointment?"

"He says will you come over to the Centre around ten o'clock."

"I shall be very glad to do so. That will give me just time to have a cigar and read the paper. I mustn't disturb those poor ladies too early."

"Miss Cowden's up at Bailtown, in the hospital."

"No, really?" Mr. Ormville was surprised. "Prostrated? I'm sorry to hear it.

Her brother's death must have been a great shock to her."

"She near died, last night. She got poisoned with morphine."

"Good Heavens! How did that happen?" Mr. Ormville put on his Oxford glasses, and peered at Hoskins through them.

"That's part of the case. Mr. Gamadge found her."

"Who is Mr. Gamadge?"

"He's—why, he's—he's a guest here in the hotel."

"I don't quite understand you, Mr. Hoskins. How did this Mr. Gamadge come to find her? And how did she come to be poisoned by morphine?"

"Mr. Gamadge was passing, and he saw that the door wasn't locked, so he went in."

"Dear me. The place seems even more informal than I thought this morning. You say this hotel guest went into Miss Cowden's room, because he found it unlocked? Really."

"Well, she kept it locked on account of being so scared of this Atwood. Mr. Gamadge told her to, and he put me in the opposite room."

Mr. Ormville leaned back in his chair, and gazed steadily at his *vis-à-vis*. Hoskins hurried on: "Only, last night this Atwood was shot and killed up at Seal Cove, so it wasn't him put the morphia in the medicine."

"Arthur Atwood was shot and killed, last night?"

"Yes, Mr. Gamadge found him."

"Mr. Gamadge appears to be practically ubiquitous."

"He was workin' on the case. Mrs. Barclay says she didn't put but a little morphia in the medicine, though. I went down to their house with them, last night, and got the bottle. Doctor Baines told me to. Mrs. Barclay had hysterics, and we had to give her brandy. The bottles are over to the Centre, and they're goin' to be analysed."

Mr. Ormville opened his mouth, closed it again, took off his glasses, replaced them, and said at last: "I suppose I may take it for granted that these events have some coherence. Why was Miss Alma Cowden afraid of Arthur Atwood? I always had a suspicion that the poor fellow was a bad lot; but why should Alma Cowden lock her door on account of him?"

"I ain't absolutely certain, but I think it had something to do with her being nearly killed yesterday by a golf ball."

"A what?"

"Somebody nearly hit her with a golf ball. Mr. Gamadge was there, and he ——"

"I shall really have to make the acquaintance of this Mr. Gamadge."

"He had me watchin' the corridor. That was how I come to sign the paper she made out, givin' all the money away."

"All whose money?"

"The money Miss Cowden got, after her brother died."

Mr. Ormville's whole demeanour altered. He leaned forward, placed his elbows on the table, and fixed Hoskins with a piercing look, through his glasses.

"Am I to understand," he asked, in measured tones, "that Miss Alma Cowden conveyed, or attempted to convey, the property which she presumably inherits through the death of her brother, to a Mr. Gamadge, one of the guests of this hotel?"

"No, she didn't give it to him. She just gave it up."

"Gave it up! She cannot give it up, Mr. Hoskins; she cannot do anything whatever with it. She is an infant."

"I know; Gamadge knows the paper ain't legal. But he's goin' to hand it over to you, just the same."

"I am beginning to think," said Mr. Ormville, leaning back again, "that you are right, and that there really is a case. This is the most extraordinary story I ever heard in my life. Did the golf ball strike Miss Cowden on the head? Is she mentally unhinged, do you know?"

"No, she ain't; but I guess Mr. Gamadge thought she would be, if we didn't sign that paper."

"If he encouraged her in this remarkable attempt to tamper with the laws of property, he is unhinged himself. I don't think I can follow the thing any further until I have had some coffee."

It had arrived, and Mr. Ormville fell upon it with a highly uncharacteristic abandon. Hoskins, wondering dimly whether he had perhaps confused the situation for the old gentleman instead of clarifying it, ate hungrily and in silence. He was rather relieved when Hugh Sanderson joined them.

Mr. Ormville greeted the young man with pleasure. He liked a good appearance, good spirits, and good humour, and he had known Sanderson's family in their more prosperous days. He said:

"Sit down, Hugh, sit down and have some breakfast. Have you finished yours, Mr. Hoskins? Then, if you have business, I won't keep you."

Hoskins said, awkwardly, that he ought to be getting over to the Centre, and that he was much obliged for the breakfast.

"How will you get there? Will you wait, and go with us?"

"No, thanks, Mr. Ormville. There's a bus."

"Well, I'm greatly obliged to you for breaking all this bad news to me. Greatly obliged."

Hoskins, looking gratified, took his departure. Mr. Ormville sighed, got out his cigarette case, and said: "I suppose the man's in his right senses."

"If he's been trying to tell you what we've been through, sir, I don't wonder you doubt it."

"You must tell me the whole story; but have some coffee, first."

Sanderson ordered coffee and toast. "I can't eat anything," he said. "This last business about Miss Cowden has knocked us all out. We were up with her, walking her, you know, until all hours."

"She actually had an overdose of morphia? Mistake of Lulu Barclay's?"

"It certainly looks that way! I called up the hospital as soon as I got up; she's much better. In fact, she'll be all right, they say, in a day or so."

"You young people!" Mr. Ormville studied him, and said: "You're not too fit, yourself. I suppose poor Amby's death was a great shock to you."

"Yes, it was, sir; it was bound to come, but I found I wasn't prepared."

"Are they having the inquest to-day? I rushed up to be in time for it."

"Well, they're talking now about postponing it, or adjourning it, or something."

"Why, in the world? From what Barclay told me over the telephone, yesterday, I understood that both their man here and Ethelbert Baines say it was death from myocarditis."

"Well, yes; it was. But then they began to worry about his being down there at the cliff——"

"I should think that was for his family to worry about. If he died from natural causes, the sheriff's office has no cause to worry about the circumstances."

"That's what I should have thought; but then these other things began to happen. Alma's accidents…"

"Well, I suppose they were accidents, were they not?"

"I suppose so." Sanderson looked troubled. "I wasn't present on either occasion. I can't imagine Mrs. Barclay putting all that morphia in the medicine on purpose. Can you, sir?"

"Lulu Barclay has done many extraordinary things in her life; she may, of course, have gone completely out of her head, but I doubt it."

"And then these things began to happen up at that summer theatre." Sanderson poured out some of the coffee that had been brought him, and took a swallow of it. He lighted a cigarette, and went on: "Atwood, and that actress."

"Actress?"

"Didn't you know? One of the actresses was found dead there, yesterday morning; I was on the spot when the medical examiner got there."

Mr. Ormville leaned back once more in his chair. "That is an item," he said, "which Mr. Hoskins omitted to include in his casualty list. But I fail to see what it, or Atwood's death, has to do with Amberley's inquest."

"I think they're completely confused, sir; they have some idea that the things have some connection with one another."

"They must indeed be confused. The important thing is to get the poor boy's inquest over, and his body in Woodlawn, where it now belongs. I cannot have Mrs. Cowden and Alma kept hanging about here while they investigate all the other deaths in the vicinity. None of us had had any communication with Arthur Atwood for years."

"Amberley had, sir."

"True enough. Do the authorities here imagine that any of Amberley's relations went up to this summer theatre and shot Arthur Atwood?"

Sanderson frowned. "They've got quite a good man on the job—a state detective called Mitchell. He seems to have plenty of sense. The trouble is, Gamadge seems to have been out after Atwood's blood, and he's got them stirred up."

"Who on earth is this Gamadge, Hugh, and what has he to do with it? He sounds like a most unconscionable busybody."

"He's a friend of the Barclays. Some sort of book expert. I didn't quite get all of it, but he looks at old books for collectors, or something, and advises them whether to buy. Writes pamphlets, I think."

"Oh. He's that Gamadge, is he? I used to know his father—delightful fellow, I was always running into him at sales and at the Caxton Club."

"Gamadge is rather a nice fellow himself; I like him. How he comes to be so mixed up in this affair, I hardly know. I think he likes Alma."

"Does he, indeed?"

"And he seemed to have some idea that Atwood had got Amberley to meet him down on the cliff, night before last. Anyhow, he's been on the spot all through everything. Sounds officious, but somehow he doesn't quite give the impression of being a busybody."

"If he persuaded Alma to try to give away her brother's money, I shall think him definitely a busybody, if not worse."

"Give away—I haven't heard a word about that, sir."

"I was a little afraid that you had been inoculating her with some of those quixotic ideas of yours."

"I wouldn't presume so far."

"Well, I must certainly have a word or two with this Mr. Gamadge. I am beginning to think that I was well advised in coming up here at the earliest possible moment. I shall advise the sheriff very strongly to let us have our inquest to-day, and to hold the other ones at his leisure. If Atwood's heirs wish to engage a criminal lawyer, they may do so; but we cannot be delayed by that procedure. I shall tell the people at Ford's Centre that I shall not allow my clients to be victimised."

"Good for you, sir. Colonel Barclay telephoned, this morning—he's in an awful state, poor old gentleman, about this morphia business last night. He says the sheriff wants a conference in his office somewhere about ten o'clock. Shall I drive you over?"

"I shall be greatly obliged if you will. I hope Eleanor Cowden will not have to attend this conference."

"No, he doesn't need her, he says."

"I shall represent her interests; and then I can come back here and report to her. You must give me a full account of the whole thing on our way over."

"I'll get the car, sir."

They rose from the table. Mr. Ormville took off his glasses, folded them, put them in his pocket, and lifted his chin to stare down his high, aristocratic nose at the young man.

"Quite a mess, Hugh, my boy," he said. "Quite a mess."

"I thought you'd realise that, sir."

"It may be as well to start at once. I should like to get to the Centre in good time."

The elm-shaded streets of Ford's Centre had a cool and pleasant smell: Mr. Ormville stood for a moment, sniffing with wistful appreciation, before he entered the fine new Town Hall. Sanderson, after parking the Cowden car, followed him up to the sheriff's office—a large, freshly painted room with a clean linoleum floor and several comfortable, wooden armchairs. Mr. Ormville sat down in one to the left of the desk, crossed his legs, balanced his hat on his knee, closed his eyes, and waited on events. Being used to the law's delay, he waited patiently for some time.

The sheriff came in, introduced himself, snatched up some papers, and went out again.

The medical examiner came in, was introduced by Sanderson, shook hands, and took Sanderson away.

Colonel Barclay came in. He looked shaky, wretched, and older than his sixty-odd years. He shook hands, said it was a sad occasion and that he couldn't make head or tail of it, and sat down. He then unfolded a newspaper and buried himself behind it. Mr. Ormville remarked:

"I hope Lulu isn't letting all this get too much on her nerves."

"Prostrated. Completely prostrated," growled the Colonel.

"That doesn't sound like Lu," protested Mr. Ormville in mild surprise.

"You may not have heard that Eleanor Cowden is accusing her of willful murder."

"Nonsense. From what I have been told, Ellie Cowden must be in a state to accuse anybody of anything."

Colonel Barclay muttered "Outrage," and Mr. Ormville relapsed into philosophical silence. Fred Barclay came in, bringing with him an aura of godlike calm. Mr. Ormville blinked at him; he was always forgetting how magnificent Fred was.

"Hello, there, Mr. Ormville." The young man came over and shook hands. "Decent of you to travel up here and see us out of our troubles."

"Not at all, my boy; it's my business, you know."

"How do you like the look of us, now that you're here?" Lieutenant Barclay, in the process of lighting a cigarette, looked at Mr. Ormville over his cupped hands.

"Not at all. You seem to have been getting yourselves into the most extraordinary mess. How is Alma? Have you had any recent news?"

"I just got on to the hospital again. She's all right, or will be when she gets over the cure she had."

"Is the child pursued by furies?"

"Looks a little that way. They seem to have been using poor Mum as a medium, you know."

Colonel Barclay rattled his newspaper, but his son continued, sitting down beside the lawyer. "Many's the dose I've had out of the celebrated bottle, with a licorice gum-drop to follow. I hear Alma says she doesn't know what did happen, Mum came in and gave her the dose, and she drank it. After that, my unfortunate cousin knew no more."

"This is very awkward—or it might have been, Now, I suppose your poor mother will get off with no worse than a scolding from Eleanor Cowden."

"Aunt El's cutting up rough, you know. Very rough. I don't know what got into her. As if Mum would intentionally hurt a fly!"

"Still, of course, one doesn't want one's nearest and dearest poisoned, even by mistake. Let us hope Ellie will calm down."

Doctor Baines rolled in, and Ormville rose to greet him with a slight excess of enthusiasm.

"Glad you're here," rumbled the doctor. His broad face showed fatigue, and a certain disquietude. "We've had a bad night, as I suppose you've heard."

"It must have been bad indeed. I'm thankful to hear that the poor girl is out of danger—thanks to you."

"Thanks to that fellow Gamadge. He has his wits about him, you know."

"I am beginning to suspect it."

"If he hadn't noticed that door, and acted promptly, she would be dead, by now; like the rest of 'em."

"May I ask whether anybody has any notion how her door came to be unlocked?"

"She says she didn't unlock it. It could be opened with any flat object. I tried on ours, this morning; and my wife is now elaborating a system of strings and chairs." He sat down beside Colonel Barclay.

Lieutenant Barclay observed: "We all owe Gamadge a vote of thanks. I'm quite aware of the fact, and also of another—he gets in my hair."

Colonel Barclay rattled his paper again, this time violently. Mitchell entered, clasping a large flat parcel in his arms. He was introduced to Mr. Ormville, by the doctor; acknowledged the introduction with a short and absentminded nod; and walked over to the right of the desk. He laid the parcel down on it, cut the string with which it was tied, and put his knife back in his pocket. Ormville, observing him with some interest, thought that he too looked as if he had had a heavy night.

Sanderson and the medical examiner came back. The former went over and sat down beside the Colonel, and Cogswell took a seat near Mitchell. Officer Pottle appeared in the doorway, leaned against the wall to one side of it, crossed his feet and folded his arms. The sheriff came in, nodded all round, and sat behind his desk. After a pause, Gamadge entered, looked about him, saw that all the chairs were occupied, and was about to accommodate himself on a window ledge, when Mitchell's voice halted him: "Mr. Ormville, I'd like to introduce Mr. Henry Gamadge."

Mr. Ormville once more got resignedly to his feet.

CHAPTER SIXTEEN
Gamadge Talking

Sheriff Enos James, who was a leathery man in late middle life, with a kindly but disillusioned eye, said: "This office has reason to be obliged to Mr. Gamadge."

"And so have we, so have we. I speak for myself as well as for my clients." Mr. Ormville, surveying the rather haggard-looking young man in the well-cut grey clothes who shook hands with him unsmilingly, decided that far from being a self-assertive nuisance, the fellow was diffident, and needed encouraging. He continued: "I believe I had the pleasure of knowing your father, Mr. Gamadge. A charming person. Charming."

"Wasn't he?" Gamadge did smile at that, waited until Mr. Ormville had reseated himself, and then took up an easy position on his window ledge.

"This poor child, Alma Cowden, apparently owes her life to your keenness of observation."

"No credit to me," replied Gamadge. "I merely happened to be on the spot."

"If I used the language of the underworld," said Mr. Ormville, "which I am seldom inclined to do, I should say that Alma has every appearance of being 'on the spot' herself. We know, of course, that that is nonsense——"

"Yes, it undoubtedly is," agreed Gamadge.

"I am glad to find that one more sensible person has come to that conclusion. Why complicate the situation," asked Mr. Ormville, glancing about him with raised eyebrows, "by assuming for a moment that the golf-course incident, and now this sad mistake about the medicines, were anything but accidents?"

"Well, they weren't accidents," said Gamadge.

"Not accidents? My dear young man, you have already said that you agreed they were not deliberate attempts on her life." Mr. Ormville raised his head, the better to contemplate Gamadge disapprovingly through his glasses.

"They weren't attempts on her life," said Gamadge.

"I'm afraid I don't follow you, sir. There is really no alternative."

"Well, yes, there is, I'm afraid."

"Would you be so kind as to state it?"

"Yes. Somebody was needed to take the blame for meeting Amberley Cowden on the cliff; Arthur Atwood filled that requirement to perfection, but unfortunately somebody was going to be needed to take the blame for killing *him* — if the suicide theory didn't work out. Problem: To provide a suspect who had a motive for making away with both Cowdens and Arthur Atwood. I thought the golf-ball incident very ingenious; don't you?"

Mr. Ormville sat back in his chair and contemplated Gamadge with the air of one who has stroked the house cat, and had his thumb bitten. The tone of patronage had departed from his voice, as he asked:

"In what way ingenious? If murder was not intended, I should have thought the risk frightful."

"You're a golfer, Mr. Ormville?"

"I was."

"You must surely realise the fact that nobody could be sure of killing, or even hitting, anybody with a golf ball at a distance of a hundred yards; but a good player could *miss* killing somebody with a golf ball, and make it the deuce of a near thing, too; especially if the player didn't particularly care whether he injured the victim or not. It was a close shave, I tell you! Mrs. Cowden, whose nerves are stronger than mine, was frightened almost sick, and I don't blame her."

"You are absolutely convinced, from your observations at the time, that the affair was premeditated?"

"Oh, absolutely. Go out there, yourself, and look at the terrain, noting the line of retreat."

"Extraordinary. And the attempt with the morphia?"

"Quite simple, as planned; but there was an unfortunate complication, which almost led to fatal results. The dose had been carefully gauged; it was to knock Miss Cowden out, give everybody a scare, and place the blame where it would do most good. But by a really remarkable piece of bad luck, Mrs. Barclay had innocently contrived, by adding an extra grain of morphia herself, to make the stuff lethal."

There was a slight commotion in the room; Colonel Barclay, trembling and inarticulate, had half risen from his chair, and his son had crossed the room to him, and was patting him on the back and laughing.

"There, Dad," he said gaily. "What did I tell you? Mum's in the clear. Sit down before you fall down, and take it easy."

"I want to go and telephone to your mother."

"She's sleeping the sleep of the just. Why wake her up? I'll telephone, later."

Mr. Ormville, displaying outrage, said: "I should indeed think that Mrs. Barclay was 'in the clear'! Nobody but a fool could possibly suspect her of anything worse than—ah—a slight carelessness in matters of detail. Mr. Gamadge, have you evidence to support this theory?"

"None, Mr. Ormville; but I might call these facts to your attention: Miss Cowden's door was unlocked; but Mrs. Barclay came and went by the door that communicates with the next room—Mrs. Cowden's. In this she is corroborated by several persons, including Miss Cowden herself. Moreover, Hoskins would certainly have seen her coming out of Room 19; he has missed certain things, but he would not have missed that. Moreover, there had been a first performance on the golf course; I expected, and tried to guard against, more of the same."

"One moment, Mr. Gamadge." Ormville's bloodless detachment, as he became interested in the exposition, might well have chilled the blood of anyone present who had expected him to disdain the improbable. "You had formed a theory about the death of Amberley Cowden? You said that someone would be required to take the blame for meeting him on the cliff. Do you imply——"

"I don't imply anything, Mr. Ormville; I assert that the circumstances of his death necessarily predicate a crime. Mind you, I considered it at first none of my business; and I shouldn't have interfered at all, only..."

"Well, Mr. Gamadge?" Ormville's voice dropped into a pause so vibrant with expectation that he glanced about him at the circle of blank, expressionless faces before he repeated: "Well?"

"Well, I didn't like what was happening to Alma Cowden; and I thought she could be pulled out of the mess before the consequences got too serious. And then, when I saw the photograph of the boy's body, I didn't like the way his face had been bashed in."

"'Bashed in,' Mr. Gamadge! I understood that he had been injured when he fell on the rocks."

"Oh, no; I don't think so. I think it was done so that Sam, the night watchman at the Ocean House, shouldn't get to wondering, if by any chance he saw the body."

"Get to wondering, Mr. Gamadge? Wondering what?"

"Wondering why it wasn't the same young man that had arrived at the Ocean House the night before."

"You cursed interfering fool!" Sanderson sprang to his feet. "Do you know what you're saying! What *are* you saying? I can't make head or tail of it. Amberley died a natural death——"

"I know he did."

"Then what do you mean by saying it wasn't his body?"

"It was. But he died on the way up from the Barclays, before twelve o'clock standard time; and the young man who took his place, and left the hotel an hour later—the young man Sam saw—was Arthur Atwood."

There were faint indications of pandemonium in the office, and Pottle uncrossed his feet; but he crossed them again, as the hubbub died.

"Sit down, Hugh," said Mr. Ormville, "and let us get to the bottom of Mr. Gamadge's delusions. What is your idea of the procedure on that night, Mr. Gamadge? Have you a coherent story to tell us?"

"I have, Mr. Ormville. Amberley Cowden died before he was of legal age; therefore he could not inherit his fortune; therefore someone else had to be substituted for him, and exhibited before a disinterested witness, well after the hour of midnight. The substitute was on the spot; he had been ready for the emergency, and had driven down to Portsmouth in response to an S.O.S. from Sanderson, who sent the message in Amberley Cowden's name from the Harbour Inn. The boy had been so ill that they were taking no chances.

"Atwood arranged his alibi at Seal Cove, and left soon after eight o'clock. He followed the Cowden car, and when it stopped, and Sanderson went back and told him the boy was dead, he had only to make up, and put on the overcoat, the hat and the gloves. Amberley Cowden's face was partially disfigured, and his body thrown over the cliff; and the party proceeded to the hotel, not later than could be accounted for by the alleged illness *en route* of a very sick young man.

"Atwood never took his gloves off at all. He made the call to Seal Cove that was to avert suspicion from himself, and to identify himself further with young Cowden; he then left the hotel, impressing himself upon Sam as being at the time alive and in presumably fair condition, and went back to the rocks, by way of the beach. He replaced the overcoat as well as he could, without moving the corpse, leaving the gloves in the pocket of it, and the hat near by; found his car, where he had parked it; and drove back to Seal Cove."

There was dead silence. Then Sanderson asked, quietly: "You wish people to believe that Alma Cowden was a party to this conspiracy? You should have allowed her to die last night."

Gamadge looked at him sombrely. "She was not a party to it," he said, "until it was all but a *fait accompli.* She was in a state of shock after the sudden death of her brother, pressure was brought to bear on her, and she thought at the moment that her whole future happiness was at stake. It was, but not as she supposed; she has been wretched ever since; and not only wretched, she has been terrified. She realised almost immediately what life would be under the régime of her three accomplices; she realised that they had planned the thing long before, and she understood what they must be capable of, and what money meant to them. She realised that her life stood between Arthur Atwood and a fortune. Do you wonder that within twenty-four hours she was ready to give the fortune away?"

"God bless my soul!" exclaimed Mr. Ormville, with a start.

"Here's the document," said Gamadge, smiling. He took it out of his pocket, and handed it to the lawyer, who unfolded and glanced at it in a kind of wonder. "Quite her own idea, I assure you. She wouldn't even sleep on it, although I gave her every chance to change her mind. I know it's not any good legally, but *she* doesn't know that. Deputy Sheriff Hoskins is ready to give evidence, if necessary."

Sanderson asked, as if with illimitable patience: "You have Miss Cowden's word for this story?"

"Oh, no; she'll never tell, not while her aunt is alive, as you are well aware. I knew that, the first time I talked to her. But luckily, I didn't need her evidence."

"This is not conjecture, then, like all that about the golf ball and the overdose of morphia; splendid. All the same," and Sanderson's voice suddenly took on a harsh, bullying note, "the story isn't true, and you'll never find one fact to support it."

"Oddly enough, I found two facts; though for a while I wasn't sure I'd ever find even one. I really had an awful day," said Gamadge, "and trying to keep the car out of circulation wasn't by any means the easiest part of it."

"What car?"

"The Cowdens'. When I realised, from what you said, that you hadn't had it out since you drove it up to the Ocean House, I managed to sew it up in the hotel garage. When I heard that Mitchell had given you back the keys, I got him to put a state policeman down there, to escort you if you invented an excuse for a drive."

"And why," asked Sanderson, his face white and glistening, "shouldn't I take it out?"

"Because the wrench that you smashed the boy's face with was still in the toolbox, wrapped in a rag. It has some blood on it, and so had your raincoat, probably; but you had a chance to wash it off in the bathhouse, yesterday afternoon. It was maddening to see you taking it down there, but I couldn't do a thing; that wrench wasn't much good to me—alone."

Sanderson laughed. "I should think not. Why need I have taken that wrench up to the hotel? And why should it have had blood on it, unless Amberley had hurt his hand on it—which of course he did? Why disfigure him—since that is your disgusting idea—with the wrench, with all those rocks there to use as a weapon?"

"It's all a question of time and mist. You had no time; it was all you could do to keep the interval you spent on the road within reasonable limits, as it was. You couldn't even risk taking the wrench down and washing it off in the ocean; you merely cleaned it as well as you could in dry sand. As for using the rocks, that was impossible; there mustn't be a drop of blood up there, and you certainly didn't dare carry the body down below. Of course you never dreamed that the garageman would take the car away from you at the Ocean House door; when Sam told us about that, I realised what a blow that must have been to you. But you hadn't much cause to worry—then."

"I have no cause to worry now. You poor idiot, what do you think will happen to that evidence, as you call it, when Mr. Ormville begins to work on it? Especially since Alma Cowden will swear that the whole story is a fabrication?"

"It wouldn't stand alone; so it was lucky my poor wandering wits got a jolt yesterday afternoon, when we walked into the hotel, and I saw those incoming guests at the desk. I suddenly remembered that Sam said Amberley Cowden had gone up to the desk; what did he do that for? Could it possibly have been to register?"

Mr. Ormville remarked, thinly, "I wondered why I had to do so this morning on a piece of writing paper."

"Mitchell took the book away in the small hours, and it's there in front of the sheriff, now."

"And what," asked Sanderson, in a loud voice, "is so interesting about the register?"

"Well, I had that signed cheque of Amberley Cowden's; you didn't find it, when you took away all the other specimens of his handwriting, including the unsigned will. You destroyed them; but of course the cheque was enough. I saw, the moment I looked at the register—as nonchalantly as I could, since you were at my elbow—that the writing there wasn't his. When we got hold of Sam, he assured us that Amberley Cowden had signed."

"Handwriting!" gasped Sanderson. "We all know what happens to that sort of evidence, in court!"

"Well, this evidence is rather special. I always notice handwriting; it's second nature with me. I had seen a specimen of Mrs. Cowden's, on one of those telegraph forms on her table; I had seen a specimen of yours—that statement you drew up for the Press; and I finally saw Miss Cowden's, on that otherwise comparatively worthless document in Mr. Ormville's hand. By that time I knew that neither you nor any of the Cowdens had signed the register, and I had a pretty strong conviction, amounting to a certainty, that Arthur Atwood had done so. I thought it very characteristic; a cynical and self-confident method of insuring himself against the rapacity of his accomplices. Or should I say employers? I realise that you and Mrs. Cowden couldn't do without him; but did you fully realise the risk you ran when you engaged that extraordinary creature to help you earn such a large sum of money? He called himself a leprechaun, but I thought of him as an Elemental; more dangerous than mischievous. He signed the register under your noses, and there, almost, without risk to himself, was future proof of the conspiracy, safe as a bank, and accessible at any time to the authorities. And he killed that unfortunate actress, up at the Cove, with as little compunction or hesitation as he would have used in swatting a fly—because he was averse to paying her whatever she demanded or might demand later, for giving him his all-important alibi—the hours between eight and ten on Sunday night; the hours he needed to get down to Portsmouth. Woe to the man or woman who tried to blackmail Arthur Atwood! I shouldn't have cared to try it, myself.

"But his was a single-track mind, and it didn't occur to him that other people besides himself might end by wandering in the void beyond good and evil. When he signed that register, he signed—if you'll excuse the well-worn phrase—his own death warrant. You couldn't very well murder Sam and burn down the hotel, so you put on that porter's uniform, and drove up to Seal Cove, and shot the fellow. If you used the Barclay car, instead of taking and abandoning one of the others parked in front of the hotel, you did so to bolster up your rapidly developing case against Mr. Barclay."

"If you think anyone will believe that Mrs. Cowden——" screamed Sanderson.

"Mrs. Cowden knew nothing of your later activities; she didn't know a thing about your departure from the Ocean House last night, via the fire escape. You were dressed, as I said, in the uniform you had taken from Room 22 after you left Colonel Barclay, and before you went out and cut across to the fifteenth tee. She certainly didn't know that you were going to scare her and the rest of us half to death with that confounded golf ball. You wouldn't have pulled the trick if you hadn't seen Fred Barclay and his mother individually trying to work off their anxieties with a little solo golf.

"Well, as I say, you left the Ocean House—just after Mitchell and I did. You wore the cap and the uniform, and you carried your own bag on your shoulder—correct me if I'm wrong in any detail. You deposited the bag in the shrubbery near the basement door, and when you came back from the Cove you picked it up and shouldered it again.

"A porter, and only a porter, can hesitate and reflect, without making himself conspicuous, before a bedroom door. You stopped a moment before Miss Cowden's, on your way back to your room; long enough to slide back the latch with a flat object —probably a key. You wanted the door unlocked and ajar, so that it might attract attention to Miss Cowden's predicament. If Hoskins or I hadn't noticed the open door, you would have managed somehow to point it out to us.

"Where did you get the morphia, by the way? Atwood had some, and he killed Miss Lake with it. Did you ask him for a supply, in case Miss Cowden needed drugging in earnest, if she reacted too desperately to the wretched situation in which she found herself? Was her fight against taking the luminal, next morning, partly an extension of the fight she had put up against taking morphia the night before? Perhaps Mrs. Cowden has some of the stuff with her still; I think she would have been glad of a dose last night, when she realised that you had nearly killed her niece —the only possible source to her of a comfortable income for life.

"And by the way, Colonel, was Mrs. Barclay's knitting bag out of her possession at any time yesterday?"

The Colonel hesitated. Then, avoiding Sanderson's wild eyes, he said: "Yes, it was. She left it on the beach."

"Was Mr. Sanderson there when you went off?"

"Yes, he was. He called up later, and said he'd found it, and was leaving it at the Ocean House desk for her."

"It seems that we were both cultivating poise at the Ocean House desk. He must have been carrying it under the raincoat. Didn't care for that evil eye of mine."

"Barclay had access to it," Sanderson's voice came thinly.

"And none of us can swear in a court of law that Mrs. Barclay wouldn't alibi him for murder. Just so," said Gamadge. "But please don't tell us that he smeared that grease across his face, and put on that cap and that uniform, and wore them up to the Cove; because after we found them, this morning, in the lavatory—where Hoskins is sure he saw you carrying them last night, under a bath towel—we tried them on him; and he can't get into them."

"Here, hold up, Mr. Sanderson!" Mitchell hurried around the corner of the sheriff's desk, and caught hold of the young man as he slipped to the floor. "You ain't so delicate as all that. Here, give me a hand, Pottle—the feller seems to have fainted."

"Appalling," said Mr. Ormville. "Perfectly appalling." He had chosen to drive back to the Beach with Gamadge, and they were following the sheriff's car along the shady road. "I have never in my life dreaded anything so much as I dread this interview with Eleanor Cowden."

"I don't think you will have to see her, Mr. Ormville."

"My dear boy, I must see her."

"I don't think she's there."

"Not there! It would be madness for her to run away from it. Do you mean she has been warned?"

"I warned her, but I don't think she'd run. I don't believe for a moment that she'd care to live, in these circumstances."

"You think we shall find her dead—of morphia? Good Heavens!"

"Yes, I do think so."

"You took a tremendous responsibility on yourself, by warning her. When did you do it?"

"Last night, while we were working over Alma. I'd just finished a shift, and

Fred Barclay and Sanderson were dragging her through the rooms. It was all pretty hectic, a kind of a nightmare. I staggered over to the corner where Mrs. Cowden was sitting, looking like death. Her nerve was going, and I don't wonder at that. I suppose I can imagine how she was feeling; whether or not she cared much for her niece I don't know; but she'd gone through a perfect hell of anxiety and effort to get hold of that money, and keep it in Alma's hands; and to imagine it slipping away to Atwood and the Barclays through some clumsiness of Mrs. Barclay's, must have been awful.

"I stood between her and the people in the room, and I said without any preamble, for I can tell you I wasn't feeling considerate: 'Mrs. Cowden, I've seen your nephew's signature, and I've seen the Ocean House register.'

"She looked up at me in that calm way she had, but her face was like wax. She said, very quietly: 'You won't let us off?'

"I told her that I had to get Alma out of it, if I could. 'Sanderson's out of hand,' I said. 'He's run amok. He's responsible for this brutality to-night, and he's just shot and killed Atwood, up at the Cove. If you don't tear loose from him now, he'll land you both in jail, as accessories after the fact.'

"She said: 'Cowardly idiot; he's been half out of his head since Arthur Atwood signed the register. I told him it didn't matter, but he's beside himself for fear of losing the money. I can't tear loose from him, as you very well know. Well, thanks for telling me, and look after Alma. Just let me alone. I want to rest.'

"And she lay down flat on Mrs. Baines' bed, and shut her eyes. She was in that plain white dress—mourning for the boy, you know. My God."

Ormville cleared his throat. "This is without prejudice: I feel inclined to hope that you were right in your suggestion," he said. "She wouldn't face it. Nobody who knew her could imagine her facing it. She's better—ah—out of it for good."

"I don't believe Mitchell or the sheriff will ask awkward questions. At any rate, not of me. Look here, Mr. Ormville, what about Alma?"

"Well…she is a minor, she was subjected to pressure from her legal guardian, and she has been in danger of her life—after putting herself on record as intending to make restitution. I don't think those French people—who must have seemed to her like semi-mythical Ho-Ho birds—will bestir themselves in the matter, since they are getting their money. Really, it was most intelligent of you, Gamadge, to make her sign that paper."

"She suggested it herself, I keep telling you."

"If the worst comes to the worst," said Mr. Ormville, "I shall have you subpœnaed as a witness for the defence."

CHAPTER SEVENTEEN
Rescue Work

Alma Cowden sat up in bed at the Bailtown Hospital, partaking of a light lunch. In spite of a slight wanness, a puffiness about the eyes, and a stringy look to her hair, and also in spite of the fact that she wore an unbleached muslin hospital shirt, fastened at the back of her neck with a safety pin, her appearance was not forlorn. She looked, in fact, better than she had done since her first arrival at the beach.

She was entertaining two visitors. Lieutenant Barclay sat on her right, mixing highballs in two graduated glasses; Gamadge, on her left, was slumped well down in his chair, hands in pockets, and eyes shut.

"Here you are." Fred Barclay handed him a glass, after giving the ice in it a final stir with a drinking tube.

"Thanks." Gamadge rose to receive it across the high bed. "You still don't seem to be in on the orgy, Miss Cowden. Too bad."

"I know all about that." Young Barclay swallowed some whisky. "Trying to get the witness tight, weren't you, so that she'd give the show away?"

"Something of the sort. Her one chance was to give it away, and I knew she wouldn't, not if she knew it."

"Well, we ought to be damned grateful to you. You know, I thought for a while that you were trying to horn in on me. I may have been a little rude."

"Not at all," said Gamadge, gravely.

"I'd better explain the whole thing, or you may get Alma and me wrong. You're such a moral guy."

"So are you a moral guy," said Alma, morosely. "Everybody seems to be moral, except me."

"Never mind, we'll save you yet." Young Barclay gave her a slow smile, and she gave him a dim one in return. "It was this way, Gamadge. It all goes back to poor Mum being so dead set on my getting some of that money. She always thought I was morally entitled to at least half of it, and that somebody must have got after Aunt Mattie—that was the one that married the Frenchman—and done me out of it. She's had a hard time of it herself, and she wanted me to have an easier one—that's all. So she concentrated on my marrying Alma. I'm afraid she got to be one of the people that just sat and watched poor old Amberley with an eagle eye, finger on his pulse, you know, praying he'd live long enough to make us all rich. It wasn't entirely her fault; the situation was enough to ruin anybody's character, except Dad's, of course.

"I don't know whether you've noticed it," continued young Barclay, "but I don't show my feelings, much."

"Something of the sort has occurred to me, once or twice," confessed Gamadge, in a serious tone.

"Especially when other people are making a great show of affection, and so on, that they don't feel. Alma's the same way. I dare say we overdid it, sometimes. We were both fond of the poor old boy, but the family made us sick. We never had any idea of marrying anybody but each other; and when I say never, of course I mean for the last couple of years, since Alma more or less grew up. But Aunt Eleanor had other ideas for her—I wasn't much of a catch, you know, and we were first cousins, and all that rot; and Mother's rage at Aunt El was such that her own methods got infernally crude. In fact, neither Alma nor I ever heard a word about anything else. I was slightly annoyed to be put in the fortune-hunter class; and it reacted unfavourably on my manners."

"I should say it did," said Alma.

"Whereupon Alma began to favour me with high-minded moral talks, and at last damned if she didn't start holding up for my admiration the noble and disinterested figure of Mr. Hugh Sanderson."

"I didn't," protested Miss Cowden, flushing. "I only said——"

"You only said *he* wasn't waiting for Amby's money. You said he loved him for himself alone, and he loved you for yourself alone, and he had refused to be down in Amby's will for more than a thousand dollars. The truth being, as I very well knew, that Sanderson was going to get an annuity. It was a dark secret; but Amberley told me all about it. You can imagine how I felt!"

"Very annoying for you," said Gamadge.

"Amberley told me, and he told Aunt Eleanor. And she told Sanderson. I knew he knew all about it, while he was going around refusing legacies. He and Aunt Eleanor were pretty thick, from the start; as business partners, of course. I suppose she must have sounded him out long ago, to find out whether he'd help her try to save the money from the French."

"Fred——" began Alma.

"I know, old girl; but you'll have to make up your mind to it—I'm never going to be sentimental about Aunt Eleanor."

"If she hadn't left that letter, I should have been in terrible trouble now."

"It was the least she could do."

"Alma is right," said Gamadge. "That letter spiked Sanderson's guns. You can't exaggerate its importance. He isn't likely to exonerate anybody. If it hadn't been for Mrs. Cowden, Alma would certainly be in a fix. But suppose you get on with the horror story."

"Well, that was the situation; Alma beginning to think that I was an unfeeling cad in my attitude about Amby, and beginning to wonder whether I wasn't a fortune hunter after all—since Mother seemed to be qualifying for the part; Aunt Eleanor telling her that I was no good, and that Sanderson was the boy for her; myself in a state of righteous indignation all round—mad at Alma, furious at Aunt Eleanor, seething at Sanderson, and hardly able to keep my temper with poor Mum; Dad fed up with the whole thing, and getting ready to think Mother and I would do about anything for money. Amberley, being no fool, had Aunt Eleanor's number, but he couldn't cope with Sanderson, and he thought Arthur Atwood was a living wonder. It would have made you sick, Gamadge, to watch them working on him.

"I hadn't seen Alma for ages; you know I'm stationed out at the back of beyond. I thought the only thing for it was a quiet talk with her, a few apologies, and one thing and another."

"That was undoubtedly the only thing for it," said Gamadge.

"I had to get her off somehow by herself; not so easy. It was a thing I hadn't had a chance to do since my winter leave. I get one month, you know, and I take two weeks in the summer, and two weeks at Christmas."

"I see."

"So on Sunday night I told the parents that I'd wash up and clear away; at which they nearly fainted. But they went up to bed, and when they quieted down I walked up to the hotel—via the golf course. It cuts off a quarter of a mile, that trail does. Are you getting excited?"

"Very much excited. How did you imagine that you would be able to get a quiet talk with your cousin at 1 a.m., in the Ocean House, with her aunt in the next room?"

"Simplest thing in the world. I know the old barn from roof to cellar, and I was planning to go up to the first floor by way of the fire escape. I knew they would be on the first floor, because of poor old Amby. I knew they'd take some time to register, and get settled; and I thought that with any luck I could reconnoitre through the glass at the end of the corridor and see what room she was in. If that didn't work, I could drop in and ask Sam for cigarettes, and get a look at the register."

"Very simple," said Gamadge.

"I was desperate," continued young Barclay, looking particularly calm. "I thought I'd wait a while, and then go and shove a note under her door. Then she could come out and join me on the fire escape. Many's the nice chat," said young Barclay, in a reminiscent and sentimental tone of voice, "that I have had, after the ball, on the Ocean House fire escape."

"I can imagine," said Alma, drily.

"While you were in kindergarten, old dear." He put out a large hand, and closed it over her arm. "And when I was at West Point. Well, Gamadge, I peered through the door, and I saw the party settling in; pretty close, too. Aunt Eleanor was right in front of me. She disappeared into Room 21, though, and I saw what I thought was Amberley's back, going into 17. Sam was shifting bags, and Sanderson milling around in and out of Room 20. I took a chance; and when the corridor was empty I slid the note under the door of 19."

"It *was* a chance," said Alma. "Suppose Aunt Eleanor had seen it? She was in and out all night."

"When you're desperate…" The two pairs of long dark eyes met, and there was a silence.

"To the deuce with eugenics," thought Gamadge, tinkling the ice loudly in his glass. "You were saying," he offered, looking at the busy gyrations of the electric fan over the door.

"Oh…Yes…Excuse us. Well, reading the note gave Alma a chance to pull herself together."

"No, it didn't," said Alma.

"I mean, you didn't scream, or faint, or fall into my arms, as you should have done. You merely opened the door, with a face as green as a lime, and said: 'Go away.'"

"You know why."

"I didn't, then. I asked, 'What's the matter with you?' And you said: 'I've been sick. Aunt El's coming. Go away.' So I went—by the back route."

"Leaving me nearly crazy."

"Well, Gamadge, the news about Amberley came in the next morning early; and, on top of that, I heard that Alma was paying the bequests in his will. I never gave a thought to Arthur Atwood; I was sure something queer had happened on this end of the line, and whatever it was, I knew that Alma must be implicated up to the neck. Paying me off like that, without a word—lumping me in with Atwood and Sanderson—it made me wild. I didn't see why she couldn't tell me all about it; she must have known I wouldn't give her away."

"You would have condoned the fraud?" enquired Gamadge. "If it's a fair question, of course."

"Well, I—no. I'd have made her drop the whole business, and—to tell you the truth, I haven't worked out what I should have done, and I don't intend to, now."

"The thing is, she was pretty sure you wouldn't stand for the fraud."

"*She* didn't stand for it long! Well, I left her a note, expressing some of my feelings, and I decided that if she wouldn't talk, I'd burst in and have a showdown with the whole lot of them. I didn't care for Aunt Eleanor, or for Sanderson, and I was beginning to be scared stiff on Alma's account."

"I saw the note," said Gamadge.

"You did?"

"Yes. I got a look at it through an operation of Deputy Sheriff Hoskins, who inserted a foot rule or something under the door and fished it out before Miss Cowden woke up and saw it."

"Well, I'll be——"

"I am totally unscrupulous. Why wouldn't you have anything to do with your cousin Fred, Miss Cowden?"

"It was Aunt Eleanor. You know, down on the road, when it happened, she and Hugh Sanderson were so kind and sympathetic, talking to me and explaining that the thing wasn't anything but a technicality. They said I was morally entitled to the money. They said it was too unjust, to make me lose it because Amby had died a few minutes too soon. They said I had a case in law. But the second I agreed to go through with it, they changed. They were like different people. It was awful down there, Mr. Gamadge."

"I can well believe that it was."

"You don't know. That fog, and Amby dying like that, and Hugh stopping the car. And Arthur Atwood driving up, and pretending he just happened to be there —I actually believed him. And then he offered to take Amby's place, so I could get the money, and the others pretended it was all his own idea. I was so confused and scared, and they all seemed to be doing it just for me. The whole thing seemed to happen in a flash.

"I said I'd do it, and then they all began to work like lightning, as if they'd rehearsed it. And I stood in the road watching for cars, and trying not to see Arthur Atwood making up—oh, how I hated him! He actually seemed to be enjoying it, as if it was a kind of play. And I was trying not to see Hugh Sanderson carrying Amby—and Aunt Eleanor holding his hat and coat, ready for Arthur Atwood to put on. I stood there, and I remembered the man driving past in the little car; I hadn't seen his face, but I knew suddenly that of course it was Arthur Atwood, and that they'd planned the whole thing, in case Amby died. And they acted as if I didn't matter at all; you could see that they were working for the money— *their* money. They knew it really belonged to them.

"It was terrible afterwards. Arthur Atwood teased them about his signing the register, and they were furious at him. And when he left, just after you did, Freddy, she came into my room—Aunt Eleanor did—and she told me I must make up my mind what to do about Hugh Sanderson. She said that I would have to give Arthur Atwood his hundred thousand dollars, if not more; but that all Hugh wanted was to marry me."

"And the rest of the million," said young Barclay.

"I told her I'd always liked him well enough, but that I couldn't marry anybody but Fred."

"That was the way to talk." Young Barclay gently patted her on the head. "Did she say she couldn't see me letting you hand over vast sums of money to Sanderson and Atwood, and even to her?"

"Yes, she did. And she said that if they didn't get their money, they'd tell you how I got it. And she said…" Miss Cowden's voice faltered.

"Go ahead." Fred Barclay took firm hold of her hand. "Go on and tell how Aunt Eleanor dropped the brick."

"I was making her angry, and of course she was dreadfully nervous and tired, but I wouldn't have known her. Even her voice was different. She said: 'I know perfectly well why you got up the nerve to go through with this; you knew Fred Barclay cares only for money, and you knew he wouldn't have you without any. Now I'll tell you something about him you don't know. He does care for money, but he wouldn't commit a fraud to get it. Can you imagine your uncle Harrison doing such a thing? In that respect, Fred's just like him.'"

"Flattering," murmured Fred.

"And she said: 'If he knew what you'd done, he wouldn't have anything to do with you. We're morally justified, but in the eyes of the law we're criminals. Remember that.'"

"Cheerful bedtime talk," said Gamadge.

"They wanted to give me morphia, afterwards. I wouldn't take it. I lay awake, and I realised what it was going to be like, tied to those three others for life. And all I could think of, at first, was that they were going to have all the money, and that Fred would never have what Amby left him. So I decided that I'd say that about giving them all their legacies so Fred could get his, and the others couldn't object."

"Very clever of you," said Gamadge.

"But Fred wouldn't take his share." Alma Cowden's eyes filled with tears. "And that night I began to wonder whether Arthur Atwood wouldn't kill me, somehow, and get five times a hundred thousand dollars. He had been saying: 'I've taken a bigger risk than you know anything about, and I've done most of the work, and you couldn't have worked it without me. Why do I get this measly hundred thousand?' You don't know how he frightened me."

"I know how he frightened Sanderson," said Gamadge.

"So I thought I'd give the money up, and then perhaps Fred—perhaps somebody—I thought Mr. Ormville might help me to go away somewhere and work."

"In other words, you had, as your aunt said, acquired the money in order to acquire this paragon here; and that's all you wanted it for."

"Silliest idea I ever heard of," said young Barclay.

"It wasn't only that." Alma Cowden looked unhappy.

"I know it wasn't," Gamadge told her, smiling. "A more miserable conspirator than yourself I never encountered. You simply didn't like the set-up, once you began to think it over. Well, Ormville is going to wangle you out of the jam, if he hasn't done it already. Mitchell is co-operating."

"I always liked Mr. Ormville. But won't it ruin Fred's career in the Army, if he marries me?"

"Ormville will tell the Army that you were kept under drugs, or something, and didn't know a thing that was going on. Your aunt's letter says plainly that you were under duress. Leave it to Ormville."

Fred Barclay said: "The parents want to see you, Gamadge, and express their appreciation."

"I'm sure I don't know what for."

"They're a little foggy about it all, but Mother has a vague impression that you saved her from a long term of imprisonment, and me from the gallows."

"Tell her they don't hang people in Maine."

"And they want to know how you got on to the thing, in the first place. So do I."

"That's hardly worth telling. It was simply that from the beginning Mitchell and I looked at the case from opposite points of view. Being a policeman, he kept wondering whether Amberley Cowden hadn't been killed for his money; being an idle dreamer, I kept wondering whether he had ever lived to get it, and thinking how unfortunate it would have been for his family if he hadn't.

"From that, the next step was to wonder what they could have done about it, if anything, if he had died too soon. Nothing, obviously, unless the circumstances permitted, and unless there had been a substitute at hand. I didn't more than play with the idea until I heard—almost immediately—that the supposed Amberley Cowden had actually wanted Sam to see him in the lobby. Instead of leaving secretly, he had left openly; and had fixed his presence there—well after midnight, standard time—on Sam's attention.

"I ceased to play with my fantastic idea; I began to consider it seriously. A substitute would have to be a young man of Amberley Cowden's general build; he would have to make up convincingly, and play a part; and he would certainly wear gloves. Nobody at the Beach seemed to fill the first requirement; how about Atwood? I went up to the Cove to see Atwood, and I was convinced.

"But I couldn't say a word to Mitchell, or interfere in any way, because of Miss Cowden. She was undoubtedly struggling with the problem, and trying as best she could to undo what had been done; I couldn't possibly ruin her chance of getting out from under. My only hope was to get some kind of statement from Mrs. Cowden, exonerating her niece. I meant to bring pressure to bear; and, thanks to Sanderson's activities, that was easy. But not pleasant… Well." He rose, and held out his hand. "Good luck to you both. I suppose you'll all be getting back to New York as soon as you can. I shall look forward to seeing you there."

"And I don't believe we shall be coming back to the Old Beach again. But you will—lucky dog. Look here, Gamadge—wait half an hour or so; I'll go back with you, and we'll have some bridge with the parents. They need cheering. Poor Mum spends all her time thinking of how to impress upon the world that Aunt Eleanor wasn't a blood relation."

"Some other time; I'm booked this afternoon. I still have that foursome with the Macphersons."

Made in the USA
Monee, IL
01 September 2025

24743376R00083